T5-AOK-837

CLOWNS
AND CLOWNING

illustrated by
**Kim Blundell,
Fiona French,
George Thompson**

First published 1978
Macdonald Educational Ltd
Holywell House
Worship St
London EC2

©Macdonald Educational Ltd 1978

ISBN 0 356 05559 0

Printed and bound by
New Interlitho, Milan, Italy

Contents

What is a clown?	4
Eastern clowns	6
Greece and Rome	8
Make clown masks	10
In the market place	12
Clown legends	14
More legends	16
Court jesters	18
Clowns in plays	20
The Italian clowns	22
Clown in England	24
A Harlequinade to act	26
The first circuses	28
Sequins and spangles	30
Clumsy auguste	32
Make clown eggs	34
Paint your own face	34
Auguste clown costumes	36
White-face clown costumes	38
Clown costumes to find	39
Circus clowns	40
Tricks and routines	42
Pompoms and ruffles	44
Great clowns of the past	46
Famous clowns of today	48
Clown acrobats and jugglers	50
Clowning families	52
Clown exercises and a clown band	54
Clowns in films	56
Clown routines	58
Today and tomorrow	60
Index	62
Acknowledgements	63

CLOWNS
AND CLOWNING

by

Carol Crowther

additional activities by
Chris Harris

Macdonald Educational

What is a clown? You watch him perform in the circus ring, theatre or on television. You laugh at his merry antics. But do you ever wonder what sort of person the clown is, under his bright costume and make-up? Why should he spend his life making people laugh? Where do clowns come from? Why do we need clowns at all?

The history of clowning stretches back over hundreds of years. Each part of the clown's strange appearance and antics has been developed over the centuries, and every society and nationality in the world has had its own clowns and funny men.

That is what this book is all about. Here you will find out something of the long and exciting history of the clown from the time of ancient China to the laughter-makers of today. You'll find out about the different kinds of clowns, their make-up, costumes and tricks. You'll learn how to become a clown yourself—how to design your own costume and make-up and make all you need for your own comedy act.

People have always needed laughter to take their minds off their problems. The clown's first job must be to make his audience laugh. But a good clown can do much more than that. Some people think that the best subjects for jokes are things that are very serious. Suppose, for example, there was something that frightened you. If you were able to laugh at it, then perhaps it wouldn't seem so frightening after all.

The clown always seems to find himself in difficulties. Everything he does seems to go wrong, but he never despairs and he never gives up. His problems are ridiculous versions of the problems that we have to face in real life. The clown overcomes his own problems and so he shows us that we can overcome ours.

The clown isn't a handsome hero, nor is he necessarily a very good person. He may be vain, greedy, selfish, cowardly or stupid, but he is still lovable. He shows us our own faults, and makes us laugh at them. He doesn't allow us to take him or ourselves too seriously.

The Emperor forebade the Mint to make any coin smaller than a 10-yen piece—a whole day's pay to a peasant. No one dared to tell him he was wrong—except the clowns! One acted as a shopkeeper selling drinks, the other as a customer who wanted a drink costing 1 yen. But there were only 10-yen coins! It was only fair to give the customer 10 drinks. With great difficulty he drank them all. 'It's good we aren't made to use 100-yen pieces,' he said. 'I'd have burst.' The Emperor laughed —but the next day he ordered 1-yen pieces to be made again.

Eastern clowns

The first clowns we know about were at the court of the Chinese Emperor 4000 years ago. Like clowns throughout the ages, they were allowed to say almost anything they liked, even to the Emperor. Sometimes they could even use their popularity to change royal decisions, but they had to be careful not to go too far. There are many stories of how clowns were able to help the ordinary people. The most famous was the jester YuSze, the court clown of the Emperor who had the Great Wall of China built, Emperor Chiiu Shih Huang-ti. The Wall was over 2480 kilometres long. People say that every metre of it cost a human life. But when the Emperor inspected it, he thought it looked rough. 'It must be painted,' he said. Everyone was shocked. It would mean years of work and many more deaths! But no one dared to say this. No one, that is, except the clown YuSze, who made such a joke of the Emperor's plan that he abandoned the whole idea. You can see another of these famous stories shown in the picture on the left.

For over 1000 years in other parts of the East —in Burma, Malaya and South East Asia, clowns took part in many of the plays, even the religious ones. They acted as attendants to the actors who played the princes and princesses. They were called 'Lubyet', which means 'frivolous men'. The royal characters walked under huge, richly-ornamented parasols. When the clowns carried these parasols they never did it properly. They turned them upside down, tripped over them or generally made a nuisance of themselves.

Malayan clowns were called 'P'rang'. They wore ugly masks with bulging cheeks, heavy dark eyebrows, and enormous turbans, so as to look as frightening as possible.

Some of the finest Asiatic clowns came from Bali. The two most popular characters who are still seen today are called Penasar and Kartala. Penasar is always worried and flustered, and determined to be on his best behaviour. His brother, Kartala, never gets anything right.

Greece and Rome

From about 700 years ago in ancient Greece, clowns took part in the stage comedies. After a serious tragedy had been acted, the clowns would perform their own funny version of the story, in which all the heroes would be shown up as fools. One of their favourite targets was the hero, Hercules. One clown would pad out his costume until he was as round as a barrel. Then he would waddle around crying 'I am the Great Hercules!' and pretend to eat and drink enormous amounts. The clowns acted scenes showing that all Hercules' feats of strength and daring had really happened by accident.

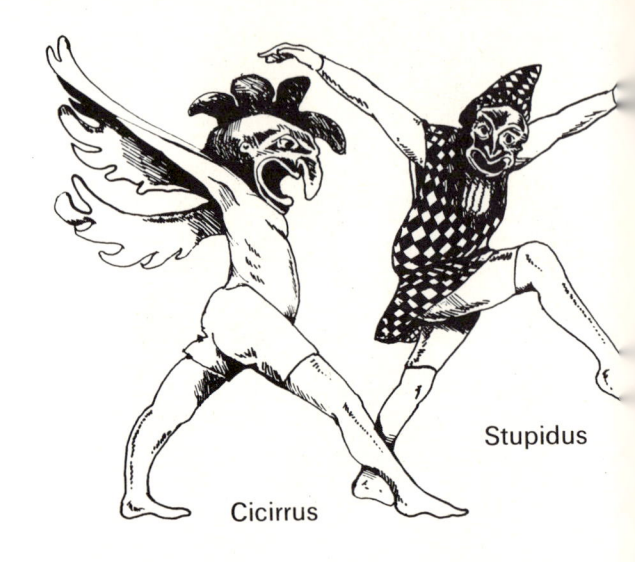

Cicirrus

Stupidus

Greek clowns made fun of the heroes and characters in the serious tragedies. Notice their enormous masks.

Below: Roman clowns also wore great masks. On the far left you can see Cicirrus, wearing the coxcomb on his head.

The ancient Romans had several kinds of clowns, too. One was called a 'Cicirrus'. He wore a coxcomb on his head and made people laugh by flapping his arms like wings and crowing like a cockerel. There was also the 'Stupidus'. He wore a long pointed hat and a costume made up of patches. He kept making mistakes and muddling up the story. The other actors pretended to be annoyed and knocked him about to make the audience laugh even more.

Roman clowns were sometimes more than just laughter-makers. The ancient Romans worshipped many gods. Everyone had to give gifts of money or animals to these gods (it was called 'sacrificing to the gods'), or they were thought to be a traitor to the state. A law was passed sentencing all Christians to death unless they would sacrifice to the Roman gods (whom they did not believe in). One Christian paid a clown called Philemon to impersonate him at the temple and make the sacrifice for him. Philemon thought it would be a great joke, but as he reached the altar he turned away. 'I cannot sacrifice', he said, 'I am a Christian.' When people saw who it was, they laughed, but the clown meant what he said. He was taken to the governor, who begged him to change his mind because Rome did not want to lose its most popular clown. But Philemon refused, and so, to the grief of the whole city, he was executed.

So Philemon died for his faith, and the courageous clown was made St Philemon.

Is your mask face a happy one? Or is it sad, jealous, mean, shy, young or old? Practise standing and moving in a way that matches your mask.

Make clown masks

You will need:
Some stiff paper or card, rough paper, scissors, elastic, gummed paper or sticky tape, paint and brushes or crayons and felt pens. Look through this book for ideas of different masks to make. The instructions below are for either a full or a half mask.

Pattern for half mask

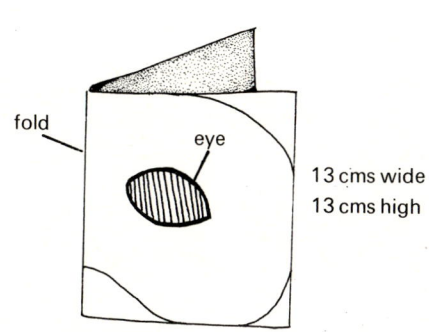

fold — eye
13 cms wide
13 cms high
keep pattern folded when you cut it out

Pattern for full mask

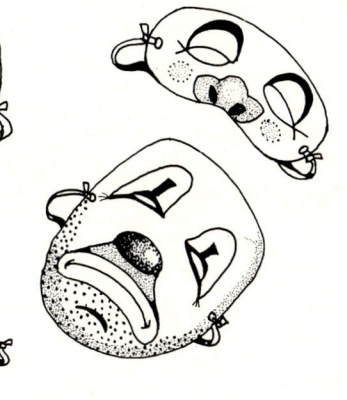

fold — eye — nose
25 cms high
13 cms wide

triangle on full mask:
25 mm base to point
20 mm across base

triangle

1. On folded paper draw the holes for the eyes and the outline. Test it against your face to see if it fits.

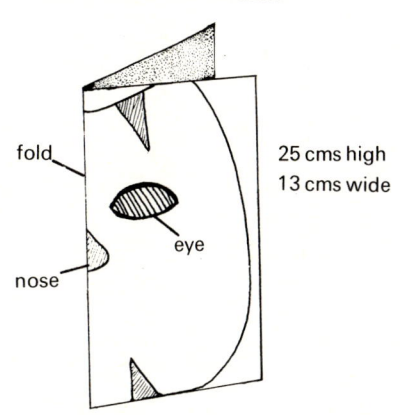

2. Cut out the mask and eyes. Don't forget the hole for the nose, and the triangles on the full-face mask.

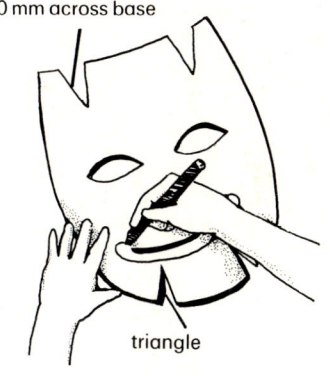

3. Open the paper pattern out. Experiment with different mask designs and colours. Look in this book for ideas.

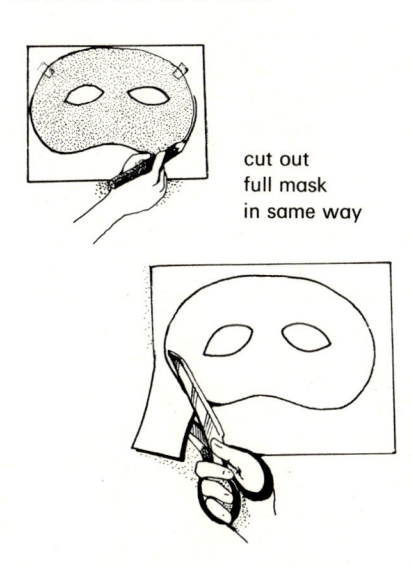

cut out full mask in same way

triangle edges held together on full mask

sticky tape — holes
elastic — sticky tape
finish half mask in same way

4. Lay the paper pattern on stiff card or paper. Draw round the shape, including eyes and nose. Remove it and cut out the card mask. Paint or draw on your design.

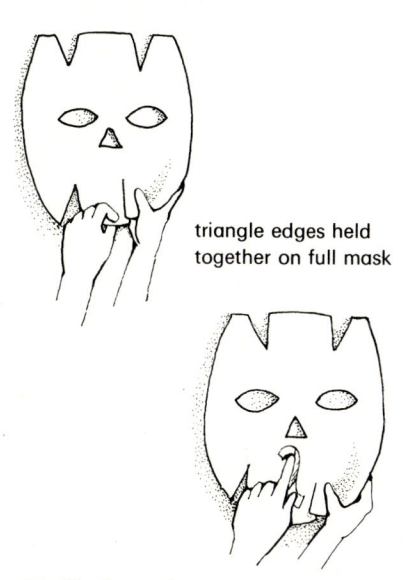

5. Pull the edges of the triangular cutouts together. Tape them together with sticky tape. Do this with all four. The forehead and chin of your mask will curve.

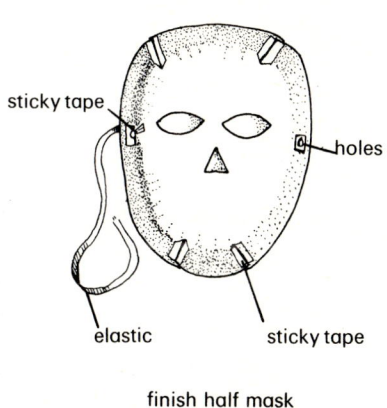

6. Stick a piece of sticky tape or gummed paper on the back. Make holes. Thread a piece of elastic through and knot it at each side. This will keep the mask on your head.

In the market place

When the Roman Emperor became a Christian, he decided that theatres should be closed and so clowns had to travel the country giving performances wherever they could. The most important event in country districts was the fair. It lasted for days or even weeks, with people buying and selling, or just watching all the entertainers who performed there.

In Germany and Scandinavia, these entertainers were called 'gleemen', and in France 'jongleurs'. There were story-tellers, ballad singers, musicians, strongmen and wrestlers, acrobats and jugglers, and animal trainers with performing bears, dogs and horses. They even had hares who had been taught to drum with their paws!

The entertainers wandered from fair to fair and even country to country, performing in market places or village greens. At special times of the year, such as Christmas or feast days, groups of 'mummers' would travel from village to village to perform folk dances and plays.

Mummers in an English market place.
On the left you can see the clown, keeping the audience out of the circle while St George fights the Turkish Knight. Below is a strange animal called a 'hobby-horse', more like a monster or dragon. It dashed about snapping at the audience. Next to the hobby-horse is Betsy, who was a man dressed up in woman's clothes. Betsy would throw her great skirts over people in the crowd, which was believed to bring them luck.

The dancers had masks or faces blackened with soot; some wore animal skins or strange costumes made from leaves; they had bells round their legs and carried handkerchieves or wooden staffs. They danced to music from a pipe, a tabor or a bagpipe.

Besides the dancers, the main character was the clown, who carried a balloon on a stick to hit people in the audience! His job was to clear a space for the mummers to perform in. He often carried a broom to sweep people out of his way, shouting 'Room! Room! For me and my broom! Give me some room to rhyme!'

The mummers performed plays which had been handed down from one generation of people to another. Stories about Robin Hood and Maid Marian or about St George and the Dragon were most popular. As time went by, the words of the play were muddled up, until St George didn't fight the 'Turkish Knight', but the 'Turkey snipe'! The audience didn't mind! The story was still a good excuse for clowning.

13

Clown legends

There are many legends about clowns who became famous long ago. Sometimes it is very difficult to tell whether the clown ever really lived or whether the legend is really a mixture of stories about many different people who became well-known for their humour, jokes and tricks. Perhaps these people even lived at quite different periods of time, but have become jumbled together in the legend.

This is one of the most famous legends. In the 14th century, the great soldier Tamburlane conquered an empire which stretched from Greece to India. He was so powerful that people flocked to his court looking for work.

One day a funny little man wearing a huge white turban applied to Tamburlane for the job of court clown. His name was Nasr ed-Din, and he looked so comical that Tamburlane agreed to give him a trial. He decided to ask Nasr ed-Din some questions, and if the clown could not answer he would be put to death. Not only did Nasr ed-Din answer all the questions but he gave such funny replies that Tamburlane gave him the job of court jester straight away.

Like most jesters, Nasr ed-Din was allowed to say and do very much what he liked with the Emperor. One day while shaving, Tamburlane caught sight of his reflection in the barber's mirror. His face looked so old and ugly that Tamburlane burst out crying. His courtiers thought that they had better show some signs of sorrow, and they wept too. After two hours Tamburlane stopped crying, and the courtiers stopped too, all, that is, except for Nasr ed-Din, who still wept bitterly.

'What's the matter?' asked Tamburlane.

Nasr ed-Din wiped his eyes. 'Sire,' he said, 'you wept for two hours because you saw your face for one moment. I have to look at it all day.'

Nasr ed-Din's jokes became so popular that they were written down, and many are still told to this day, although sometimes his name is spelt Nasrudin. Towards the end of his life, Nasr ed-Din became a priest, but in spite of his clever humour, he couldn't give a proper sermon. On the first day he stepped into the pulpit and asked the congregation 'Do you know what I am going to tell you today?'

'No,' answered the congregation, and looked at him expectantly.

'Neither do I,' said Nasr ed-Din, and hurried away. A week later he asked the congregation the same question. This time they tried a different answer. 'Yes,' they said.

'Then I won't bother to tell you,' said the little clown.

The following week he asked again, 'Do you know what I am going to tell you?' This time the congregation were determined to get their sermon, so they answered, 'Some of us do, and some of us don't'.

'That's good!' said Nasr ed-Din. 'The ones that do know can tell the ones that don't!' And away he went.

When he died they built a monument to the little clown at Aqshehir. People still visit it. They make wishes and tie strips of cloth round the statue which represents Nasr ed-Din's famous turban. It is said that Nasr ed-Din will use his power to make sure that the wishes come true.

Can you find any stories about Nasr ed-Din, or Mulla Nasrudin as he is sometimes called?

More legends

Many countries have had their favourite clown figures. In Germany there was Till Eulenspiegel, who was a legendary practical joker. According to the stories he was born in Saxony. Although his parents were very poor Till refused to do any work, and spent his time practising tight-rope walking. He thought himself so clever that one day he fixed his rope over a stream. His neighbours decided to teach him a lesson, and when Till was right above the stream they cut the rope.

Till was determined to have his revenge. One day he told his neighbours that he had a wonderful trick to show them, but that he needed to borrow their shoes. He tied all the shoes together and hoisted them up into the air. 'Now watch carefully,' he said. As the crowd gazed into the air, Till cut the cord and all the shoes fell down upon them. By the time they had sorted out their shoes, Till Eulenspiegel had escaped. He travelled all over the country causing trouble wherever he went. Sometimes he rode a horse, and carried an owl and a mirror, for his name meant 'Owl-glass'.

Once he told the Prince of Marburg that he would paint a splendid mural. For days and days Till pretended to be busy, then finally he said the painting was finished. In fact he had done nothing, and the walls were bare. But Till explained that his painting was magic and could only be seen by people who had no guilty secrets. Nobody dared admit that they couldn't see a thing. Then the Prince realised that he had been tricked; but Till Eulenspiegel had already escaped and was on his way to cause more mischief elsewhere.

There was another legendary joker who was famous in the Mediterranean island of Sicily. He was called Giufa. Because he was poor he was never invited to any parties.

Then one day, his mother dressed him up so smartly that he was invited to dine at a neighbouring farmhouse. While he was sitting at the table, Giufa ate all the food he could with one hand, while pushing food into his pockets with his other hand. His host noticed and asked him what he was doing.

'You didn't really invite me,' said Giufa, 'You only invited my clothes! I think it's only fair that they should eat too.'

You can see a picture of Giufa on the right.

In England people believed that there was an imp called Robin Goodfellow.

Like Till Eulenspiegel and Giufa, Robin Goodfellow liked to play jokes on people, but as he had magic powers he was also able to disappear or turn himself into different shapes. He would rattle door-handles at night, and blow out people's candles. Then he would disappear with a loud laugh, which was the sign that he'd been up to mischief.

Robin Goodfellow is shown in the picture below.

Court jesters

In Europe during the Middle Ages court jesters were called 'fools'. Some were simple-minded, but most were clever clowns who pretended to be stupid to make people laugh. Some wore coxcombs, like the 'Cicirrus' in ancient Rome. Others wore hooded caps with long ears and bells. They wore gaudy clothes called 'motley', and carried sticks with carved fools' heads on the top, known as 'marottes', or sticks with bladders, like balloons, with which they jokingly beat people. In Germany jesters were called 'merry councillors', for their witty remarks also included good advice.

Some remarkable jesters lived in France. In 1380 one called Jehan was even asked to decide a case between a baker and a street porter. The greedy baker was annoyed that a poor man was sniffing the food cooking inside, and said that he should pay for the smell of the food. Jehan pretended to agree. He ordered the man to rattle coins in his pocket. 'Do you hear the clinking?' Jehan asked the baker. 'That's your payment. The *sound* of the money is paying for the *smell* of the food.'

Some jesters were treated as members of the family. Triboulet, jester to the French King Francis I, was even taken on military campaigns. But Triboulet was not very brave. The noise of the cannon frightened him and during battles he hid under his bed. Once he annoyed a nobleman, who threatened to kill him. Triboulet was terrified. 'Never mind,' said the King. 'If he dares to kill you, I will have him executed half an hour afterwards.' Triboulet looked at the King doubtfully. 'Couldn't you have him executed half an hour before?' he asked.

The last court jester in England was Jeffery Hudson. King Charles I and Queen Henrietta Maria were having dinner with the Duke of Buckingham. The servants carried in an enormous pie, but before the King and Queen could reach for their knives and forks, out stepped a midget less than half a metre high! The Queen made him her own jester.

The jester Jeffery Hudson arrived in a pie.
He was less than half a metre high.

A scene from Shakespeare's play 'A Midsummer Night's Dream'. The clowns perform their play 'The Comedy of Pyramus and Thisbe' for the wedding celebrations of the Duke and Duchess of Athens. The characters you can see in the picture are, from left to right: Lion, Moonshine with lantern and dog, the Prologue, Pyramus looking through the chink in Wall's fingers, Wall and the 'lady' Thisbe.

Clowns in plays

During the Middle Ages clowns did perform in the theatre, but mainly in religious plays, as 'devil' figures or 'Vices', symbolising stupidity and evil. Writers found that comic scenes in serious plays helped to keep the audience amused and even helped to explain the meaning of the story, for often the clown was a narrator. He described what the audience was about to see or explained what had just happened. If the audience was getting bored, the clown could tell a few jokes, or even dance a jig to catch their attention.

Then some writers realised that they could use the clown better as a comic contrast to the more serious characters. In Germany, writers of the 'Carnival plays' delighted in showing the foolishness of people who set themselves up as better than everyone else. The clown was just the right character to show that a wise fool could be more clever than a wise person who acted foolishly. All over Europe the clown was used in this way. In France he was called a 'Badin', and in Spain a 'Bobo'.

But many writers had thought it would be wrong to show a king and a fool on the same stage, or to mix tragedy and comedy together. It was the famous English playwright, William Shakespeare, who showed that the clown could provoke both laughter and tears, and his jokes could make the tragic happenings in the play more dramatic and terrible. At last the clown was given the chance to be as important as any serious actor in the greatest plays of all.

However, Shakespeare himself had trouble with his own clowns—Will Kemp and Richard Cowley—for they were really more interested in making the audience laugh than in saying the words that Shakespeare had written for them. They would make up the words, or 'ad lib', as they went along, adding all sorts of extra comedy, even if it interrupted the play. Kemp was famous for his dancing. He insisted on dancing a jig on every occasion. This delighted the audience, but it only made Shakespeare very angry.

The Italian clowns

In 16th-century Italy, the plays of the companies called 'Commedia dell'Arte' became very popular. The actors had only an outline of the story, and made up their own words to fit the characters. Some characters were particular favourites and appeared in every play. Each one came from a different region of Italy, and had a special costume and mask which the audience could recognise. The picture above shows the most famous characters wearing the traditional masks and costume.

From left to right you can see Arlecchino in patches, Pantalone in red, Brighella in white and green, Pulcinello in white with the pointed hat, The Doctor in black and The Captain.

Arlecchino, a greedy servant, was the most popular. His patches showed how poor he was. He was very crafty, but frequently got into trouble and was whipped. He was often the servant to the miserly merchant Pantalone, whose red trousers were known as 'pantaloons'.

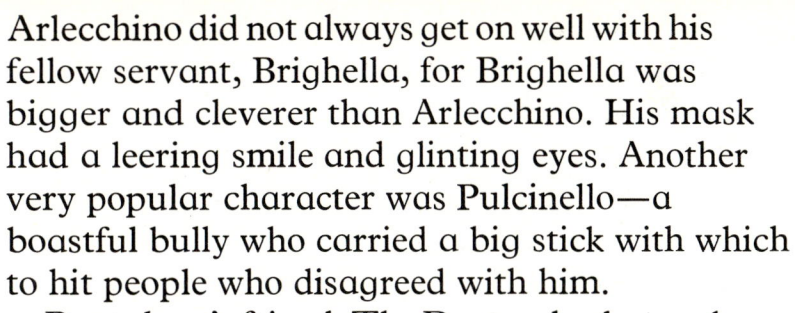

Arlecchino did not always get on well with his fellow servant, Brighella, for Brighella was bigger and cleverer than Arlecchino. His mask had a leering smile and glinting eyes. Another very popular character was Pulcinello—a boastful bully who carried a big stick with which to hit people who disagreed with him.

Pantalone's friend, The Doctor, had a mask with red cheeks to show he was fond of drink! Sometimes he was a medical doctor, sometimes a lawyer or a professor. He wasn't as clever as he pretended, and would deliver whole lectures on 'He who is wrong cannot be right', or 'One who is asleep cannot be awake'! The Captain had a quick temper and looked fierce. He was always boasting about his conquests, but was really a dreadful coward. There were many other characters; the sad white-faced 'Pierrot'; the beautiful girl 'Columbine'. The Commedia dell'Arte was so popular that its influence spread through Europe and finally to England.

24

Clown in England

In England the names of the Commedia dell'Arte characters changed so that English people could say them; from Arlecchino to Harlequin, Pantalone to Pantaloon and Pulcinello to Mr Punch—the well-known puppet character of today. Pierrot changed too—his new name was just Clown, and he became the favourite, for the part was played by the famous Joseph Grimaldi.

Joseph Grimaldi, or 'Joey' as he was known, was born in 1778. He went on stage when he was only two. By the time he was 20, he was an experienced clown and acrobat. In 1806, Joey was given the part of Clown in the pantomime 'Harlequin and Mother Goose'. From the moment he stepped on stage, he stole the show.

Old pantomime always included a play about Harlequin and his friends with tricks and 'transformation' scenes. In these 'Harlequinades', Joey built strange things out of everyday objects. From vegetables he built a man. Then, using turnips as boxing gloves, he boxed with him! The vegetable man magically came to life and chased Joey off the stage. In another pantomime he dressed up as a soldier—two coal buckets for boots, candlesticks for spurs, a lady's fur muff for a helmet—and Captain Joey was ready.

The audience also loved Joey's songs, like 'Tippetywichet' and 'Hot Codlins', and even after he stopped performing they were included in every pantomime.

Although he was funny on stage, Joey was not very happy in real life. A clown's life was hard. He often had broken bones from his tumbling. One day a very tired and depressed man went to see a doctor. The doctor could find nothing wrong with him. 'You need something to cheer yourself up,' he said. 'Go and see Grimaldi, he'll make you laugh.' 'But doctor,' replied the patient, 'I *am* Grimaldi'.

Joey died 150 years ago, but his fame continues. Many of his jokes are still used in pantomimes, and in the circus, clowns are still called 'Joey' in his honour.

After Joey Grimaldi retired, Tom Matthews became the most popular clown in England.

80 years ago Dan Leno delighted audiences in music halls all over England.

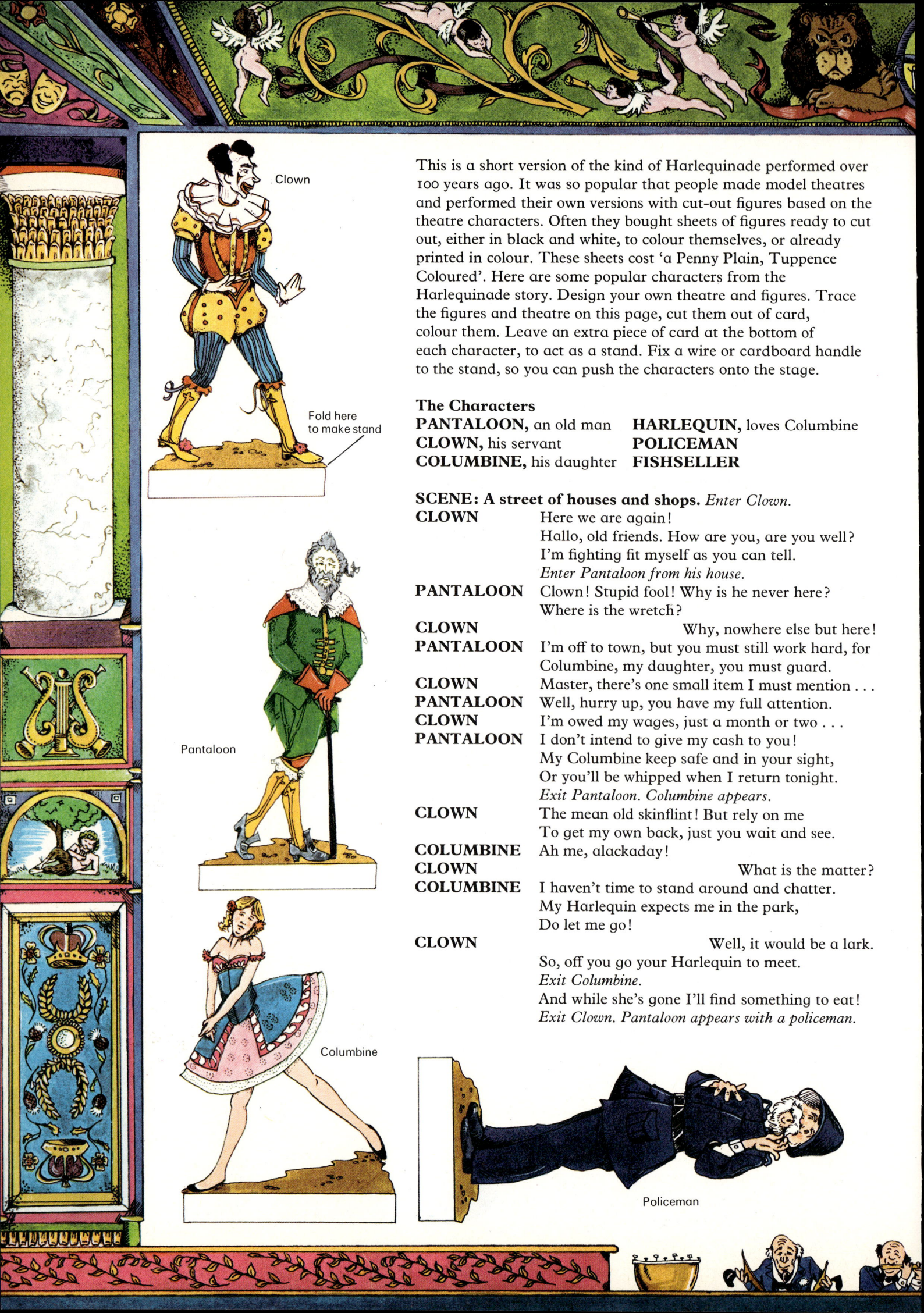

This is a short version of the kind of Harlequinade performed over 100 years ago. It was so popular that people made model theatres and performed their own versions with cut-out figures based on the theatre characters. Often they bought sheets of figures ready to cut out, either in black and white, to colour themselves, or already printed in colour. These sheets cost 'a Penny Plain, Tuppence Coloured'. Here are some popular characters from the Harlequinade story. Design your own theatre and figures. Trace the figures and theatre on this page, cut them out of card, colour them. Leave an extra piece of card at the bottom of each character, to act as a stand. Fix a wire or cardboard handle to the stand, so you can push the characters onto the stage.

The Characters
PANTALOON, an old man   **HARLEQUIN,** loves Columbine
CLOWN, his servant   **POLICEMAN**
COLUMBINE, his daughter   **FISHSELLER**

SCENE: A street of houses and shops. *Enter Clown.*
CLOWN Here we are again!
Hallo, old friends. How are you, are you well?
I'm fighting fit myself as you can tell.
Enter Pantaloon from his house.
PANTALOON Clown! Stupid fool! Why is he never here?
Where is the wretch?
CLOWN Why, nowhere else but here!
PANTALOON I'm off to town, but you must still work hard, for
Columbine, my daughter, you must guard.
CLOWN Master, there's one small item I must mention...
PANTALOON Well, hurry up, you have my full attention.
CLOWN I'm owed my wages, just a month or two...
PANTALOON I don't intend to give my cash to you!
My Columbine keep safe and in your sight,
Or you'll be whipped when I return tonight.
Exit Pantaloon. Columbine appears.
CLOWN The mean old skinflint! But rely on me
To get my own back, just you wait and see.
COLUMBINE Ah me, alackaday!
CLOWN What is the matter?
COLUMBINE I haven't time to stand around and chatter.
My Harlequin expects me in the park,
Do let me go!
CLOWN Well, it would be a lark.
So, off you go your Harlequin to meet.
Exit Columbine.
And while she's gone I'll find something to eat!
Exit Clown. Pantaloon appears with a policeman.

Clown

Fold here to make stand

Pantaloon

Columbine

Policeman

PANTALOON	I'm back because I've had a good idea,
	I've hired this policeman and he can stand here.
	Sergeant, if you catch Harlequin I'm willing
	For his arrest to pay an extra shilling.
POLICEMAN	Right you are, sir, be sure I won't go in
	Until I've caught that rascal Harlequin.
	Exit Pantaloon. Clown enters and sees the policeman.
CLOWN	Why is that policeman standing in the street?
	I think I'd better lure him off his beat.
	If he should catch a sight of Harlequin
	And Columbine, what trouble I'll be in!
	Clown exits. Enter a woman with a basket of fish.
FISHSELLER	Fish for sale, come, buy my nice fresh fish!
	Clown appears and sees her.
CLOWN	Ah, better luck than this I couldn't wish.
	He goes up to her and steals a large fish. He runs off-stage then reappears holding the fish.
FISHSELLER	Help, policeman, I've been robbed!
POLICEMAN	Come back, stop thief!
	They chase Clown off. Enter Harlequin and Columbine.
COLUMBINE	No one about at all! That's a relief.
HARLEQUIN	Now come, my love, we must no longer tarry,
	We'll get your Pa's consent and then we'll marry.
	Enter Pantaloon. He sees Harlequin and Columbine.
PANTALOON	What? Harlequin! This isn't what I planned.
HARLEQUIN	Sir, I have come to ask your daughter's hand.
PANTALOON	Never, you spangled wretch, you ask in vain.
	I never wish to see your face again.
HARLEQUIN	What? You refuse! Well, we will see to that,
	For Harlequin still has his magic bat.
	One touch and Pantaloon upside down you'll find.
	And there you'll stay until you change your mind.
	With his bat he touches Pantaloon who turns upside down.
HARLEQUIN	Do you agree your daughter shall be mine?
PANTALOON	Oh, very well.
HARLEQUIN	Then I'll wed Columbine.
	He touches Pantaloon again and he stands upright.
COLUMBINE	From this moment then let joy begin
	For happy Columbine and Harlequin.
	Enter the Clown.
CLOWN	After this tale of trouble and disaster
	Our characters live happy ever after.
	Good health and happiness be very near
	To you, until we meet again next year!

Harlequin

Pantaloon turned upside down

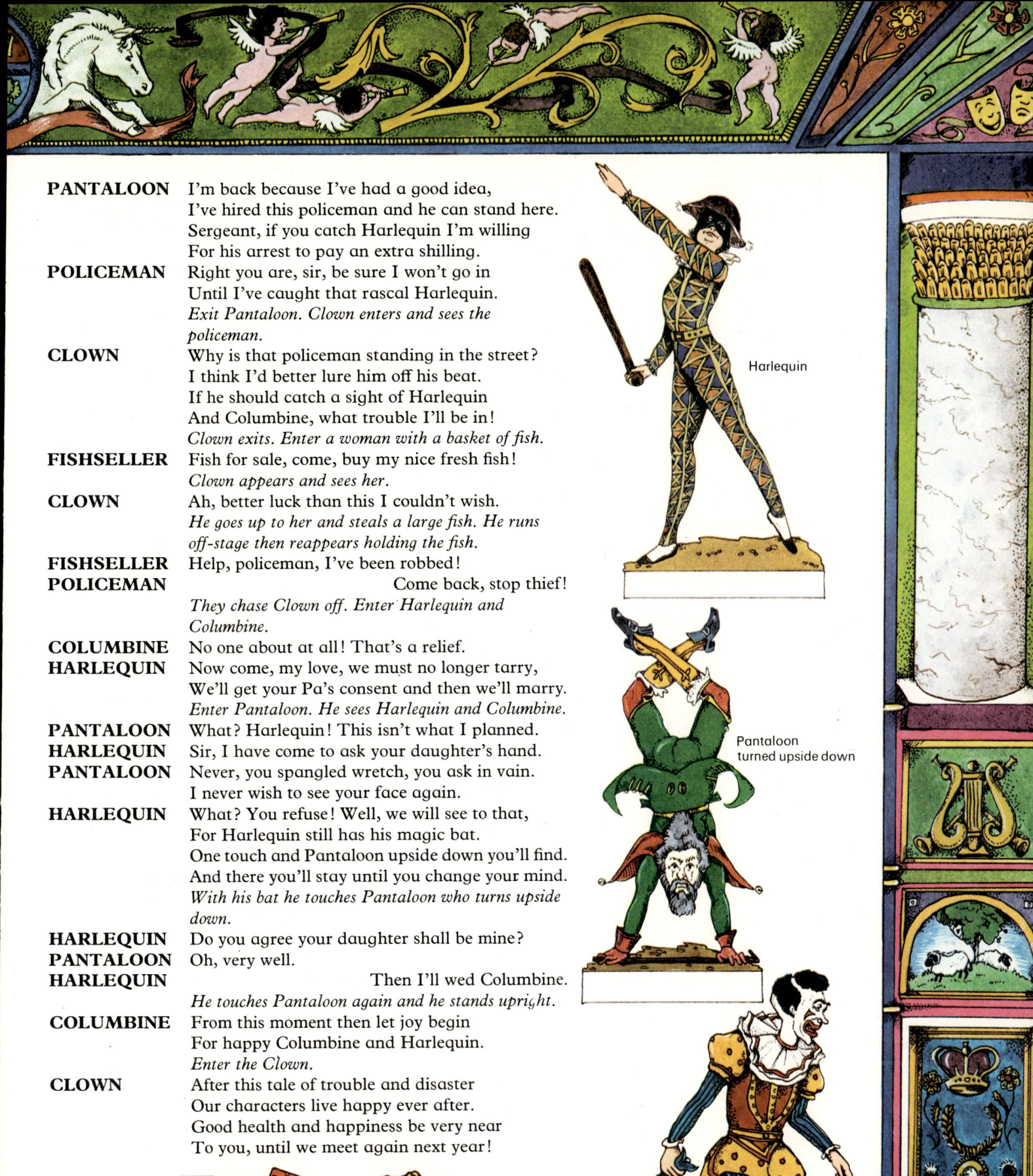

Fishseller

Clown with fish

Clowns performing in the ring at Astley's Royal Amphitheatre.

The first circuses

More than 200 years ago, in 1766, a young sergeant-major called Philip Astley left the Army. He bought two horses for £10, and with his wife's help began to give displays of trick riding. Then Astley discovered that it was easier to balance if he made the horse gallop in a circle instead of a straight line while he was standing on its back. So he roped off a circle of ground to perform in. And so the circus was born!

Astley's first circus site was in London. He hired other riders as well, but he soon found that he needed other acts besides trick riding. He added tight-rope walkers, acrobats, strongmen and trained animals. Most important was a clown called Mr Merryman, who performed a comedy riding act.

The performances were so successful that Astley was able to build a permanent circus called the Amphitheatre. He also started a circus in France in 1782; in fact Astley had 19 permanent circuses built during his life.

One of Astley's riders, Charles Hughes, set up a rival circus which he took to Eastern Europe, and in 1793 he founded the Russian circus. At the same time, a man named Bill Ricketts, who had worked for Hughes, set up a circus in America. The opening performance was attended by President George Washington. The number of circuses spread. They got bigger and bigger, until Barnum opened his enormous three-ringed circus seating thousands of people.

After Astley retired, his Royal Amphitheatre in England was taken over by Andrew Ducrow, who, like Astley, was an expert rider. His brother John was the clown, one of the greatest clowns of his time. Ducrow invented an act which circus clowns still perform. A riding act is in progress, when a member of the audience steps into the ring. He pulls the rider off the horse, and tries to mount, but is rather unsteady and keeps falling off. In the skirmish, he loses his trousers and reveals strange, gaudy underwear! It isn't a member of the audience at all, but a clown who then goes into his act with the other riders.

Sequins and spangles

Below: the splendour and elegance of a white-face clown costume worn by Charlie Cairoli Junior at Blackpool Tower Circus in England.

Right, top: the man becomes a clown. First the white make-up is added. Then the red lips and black around eyes and eyebrows.

Right, bottom: only the hat to be added and Clown Davide of England's Clown Cavalcade is ready for his act.

The first circus clown wore white make-up very like that used by Grimaldi in the theatre. The purpose of the make-up was the same, to make sure that the clown's funny expressions could be seen clearly from the back row of seats. Why did they choose a white face? Like so many things in the history of clowning it happened by chance.

The story is told that in Paris about 370 years ago there was a baker whose hobby was acting. His nick-name was 'Gros-Guillaume' which means 'Fat William', and when he walked on stage he looked like a great barrel. But William had to work very hard at his bakery. After he had shut up his shop he barely had time to rush to the theatre and get into his costume before the show started. One night he was later than usual. He didn't even have time to wash the flour off his face before he went on stage. Much to his surprise Fat William found that the audience thought he was even funnier with his big white face. Other clowns copied him. The white face has been worn by clowns ever since.

The white make-up clowns use today is more than just a coating of flour. On the white base the clown adds the touches of red and black which make the make-up his own. Each clown designs his make-up to suit his clown personality. It may take many months before the clown feels that he is happy with his make-up. Then he normally uses it for the rest of his life. An experienced clown can put on his make-up in five minutes. There are hundreds of clowns, but no two make-ups are alike.

Some white-face clowns wear loose fitting suits, like pyjamas. Others wear tightly-fitting costumes decorated with frills round the arms and legs. This costume was invented by Richard Flexmore in the 1840s. Other clowns copied Flexmore's costume and tried to improve it, adding more spangles, until every inch of the costume was covered with glittering sequins. A spangle costume often has over 30,000 sequins on it, and costs several hundred pounds. It is often the clown's prize possession.

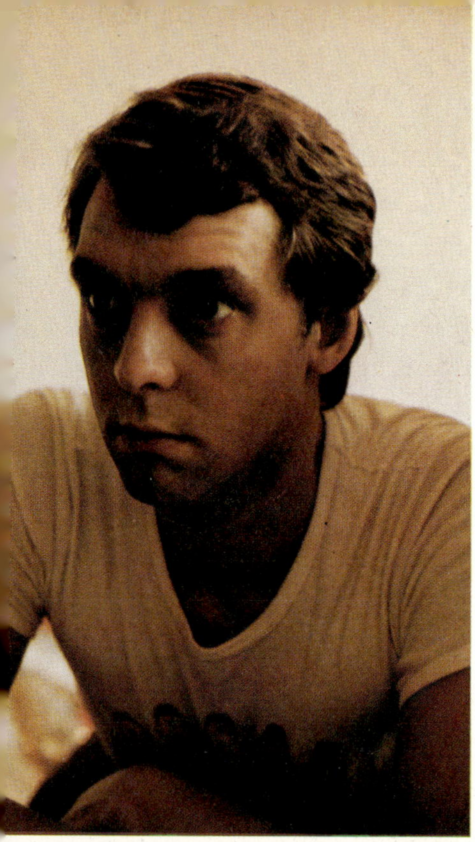
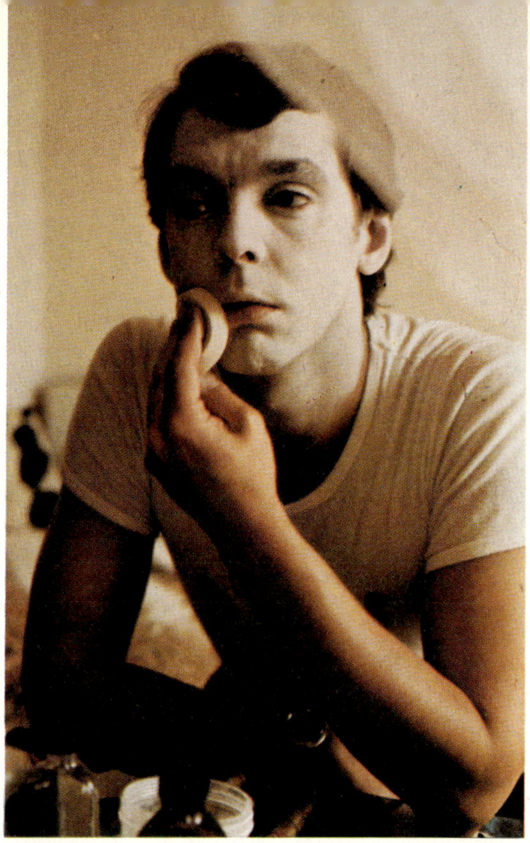
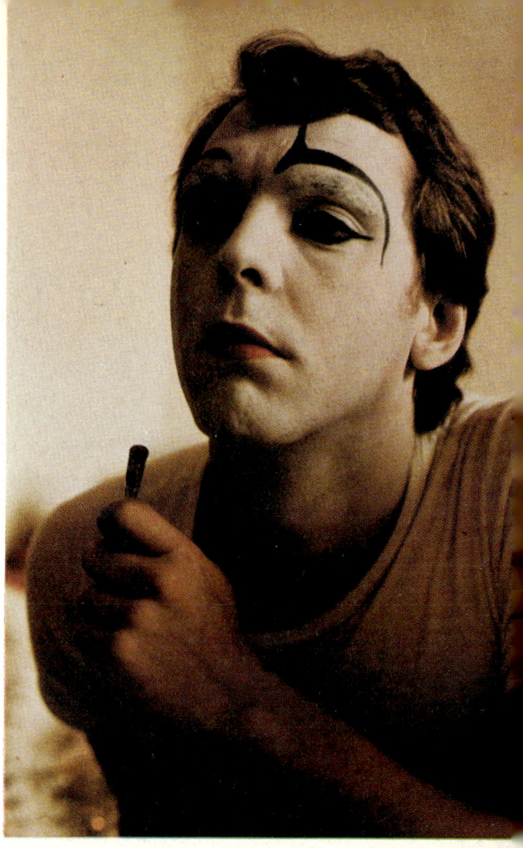
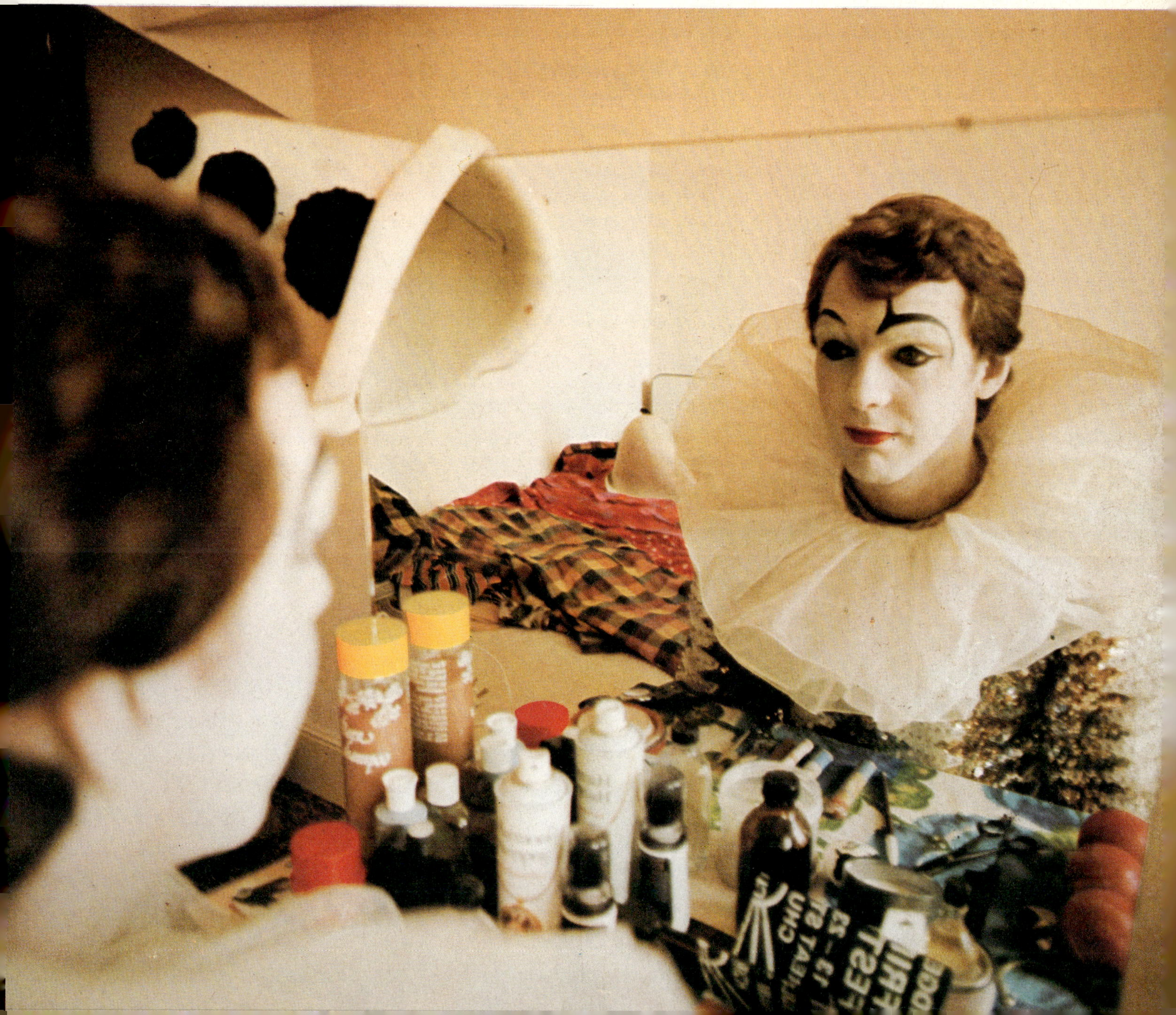

Clumsy auguste

Below: and bottom-left: one of the best-loved of all augustes was Coco, who was born in Russia in 1900. He ran away to the circus when he was very young.

100 years ago in a circus in Berlin, a young acrobat called Tom Belling had been barred from the ring for a month because he played practical jokes on his fellow performers.

Poor Tom missed the noise and bustle of the circus. He found an old wig, an old coat which he put on back to front, and he tiptoed down to the ringside, sure that nobody would recognise him. He was so busy watching the circus that he didn't notice someone standing beside him—the circus owner. The circus owner laughed, and slapped Tom on the back. The young man fell into the ring. The audience thought it was all part of the show and roared with laughter. They shouted 'Auguste! Auguste!' a German nick-name for a clumsy person. The audience enjoyed the fun so much that Tom repeated the act night after night. So a new kind of clown was created, and even today he is still called an 'auguste'.

With the circus he travelled all over Europe. Later he joined Bertram Mills Circus and came to England. When something startled him his orange hair stood up on end.

Below: three different auguste clowns of the Clown Cavalcade troupe in England. From left to right, Antonio, Bazzo and Zappo. Each one has different make-up.

Augustes now appear in circuses all over the world. They wear crazy versions of everyday clothes which are either much too large or much too tight. Their suits have brilliant colours and wild patterns and checks that make you feel dizzy. Sometimes they have long shoes with toes more than half a metre long, or boots so big they look as if they were left behind by a forgetful giant.

The clumsy auguste and the elegant white-face clown are splendid partners. The white-face clown is nimble and graceful, but the auguste is always dropping things and tripping over. It is the white-face clown who is the boss, and the auguste who comes off worst in any argument. When the clowns are fighting over a bucket of water you can be sure that it is the auguste who will get soaked, and if there are any custard pies flying around the poor auguste will be the one who gets it in his face.

Make clown eggs

When a clown wanted to record his make-up, he used to paint it on an egg-shell. These eggs were preserved, and no other clown could copy a make-up once it had been registered on an egg.

You will need: eggs, pin, bowl, paints, colourless varnish, a tissue.

1. Take a large, smooth egg (white for a white-face clown, and brown for an auguste). Make a small hole in each end with a pin. Hold the egg over a bowl and blow into one hole. The inside of the egg will pour out the other end.
2. Wash the egg carefully and leave it to drain on the tissue. When it is dry, stick a piece of paper over each hole to strengthen the egg.
3. Lightly mark out the face with a pencil. Then paint it. Be careful not to hold the eggshell too tightly, or it might crack.
4. When the paint is dry you can paint it with a transparent varnish like colourless nail varnish.

Paint your own face

1. Decide whether you want to be a white-face clown or an auguste. Look at your face in a mirror. Frown. Feel the creases this makes on your forehead. Now pull a funny face and find the creases this makes all over your face. Join up the creases to make shapes. Use these shapes when you design your make-up, rather than just paint shapes on anywhere.
2. With an eyebrow pencil or soft drawing pencil gently draw on the main shape of your make-up. For a white-face clown the eyebrows are most important. For an auguste it is the shape of the eyes and mouth. The white-face clown has dainty eyes and mouth, the auguste usually large eyes and an enormous mouth.
3. Traditionally, clowns use red, white and black, because these colours can be seen by an audience sitting some distance away in a large theatre or circus. But you can experiment with other colours.
4. Use red lipstick, white stick eyeshadow and black eyebrow pencil. For a white-face clown, dust your face all over with talcum powder before you mark on the final shape. For an auguste, mark the shapes straight on to your own skin, then colour them in.
5. Keep the design simple. Check that the make-up looks good when you move your face as well as when you keep your face still.

Experiment till you find the make-up that suits you. Even professional clowns may take weeks to get their make-up just right. Then, as they get more experienced, it is simplified until it can be put on in just a few minutes.

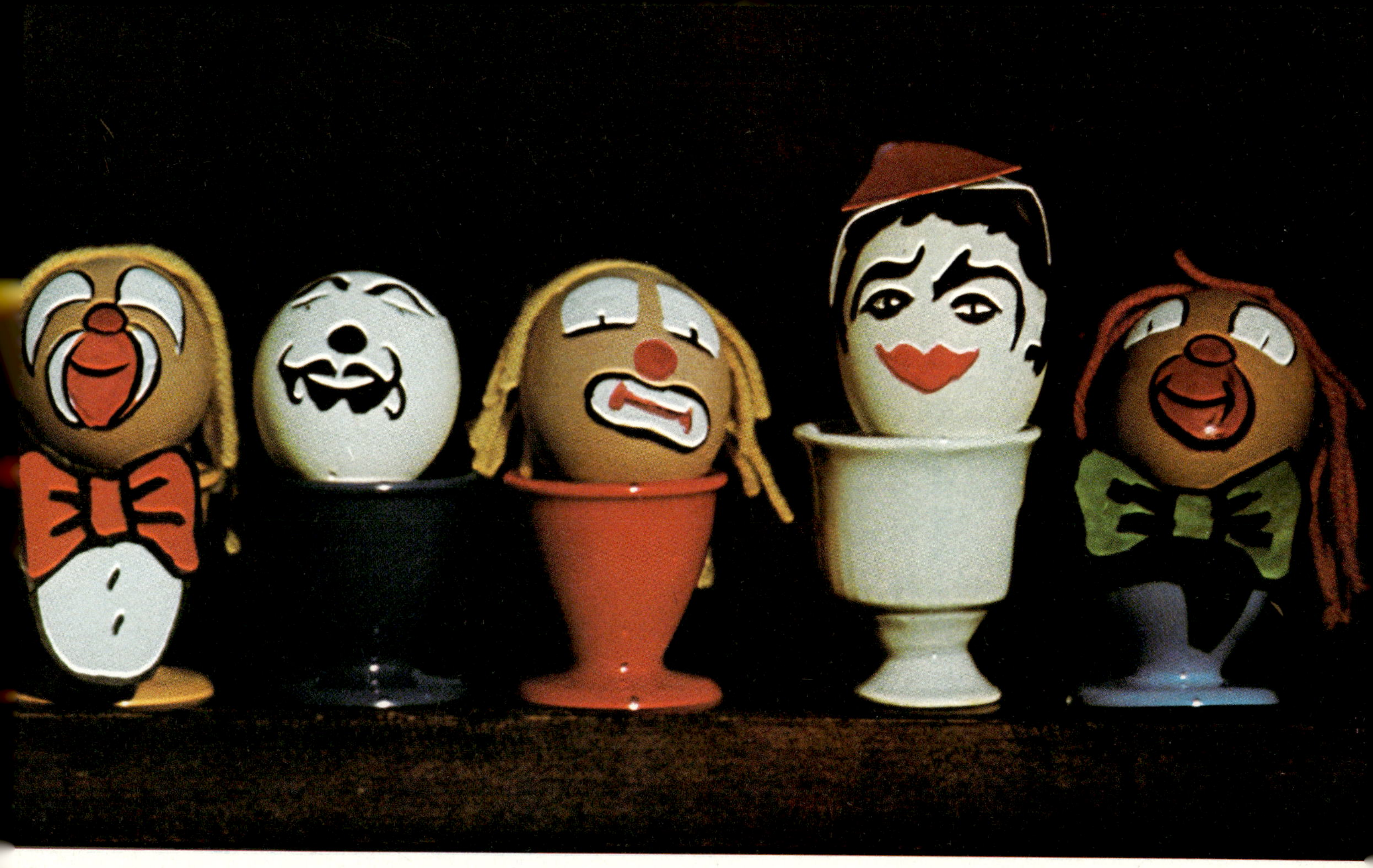

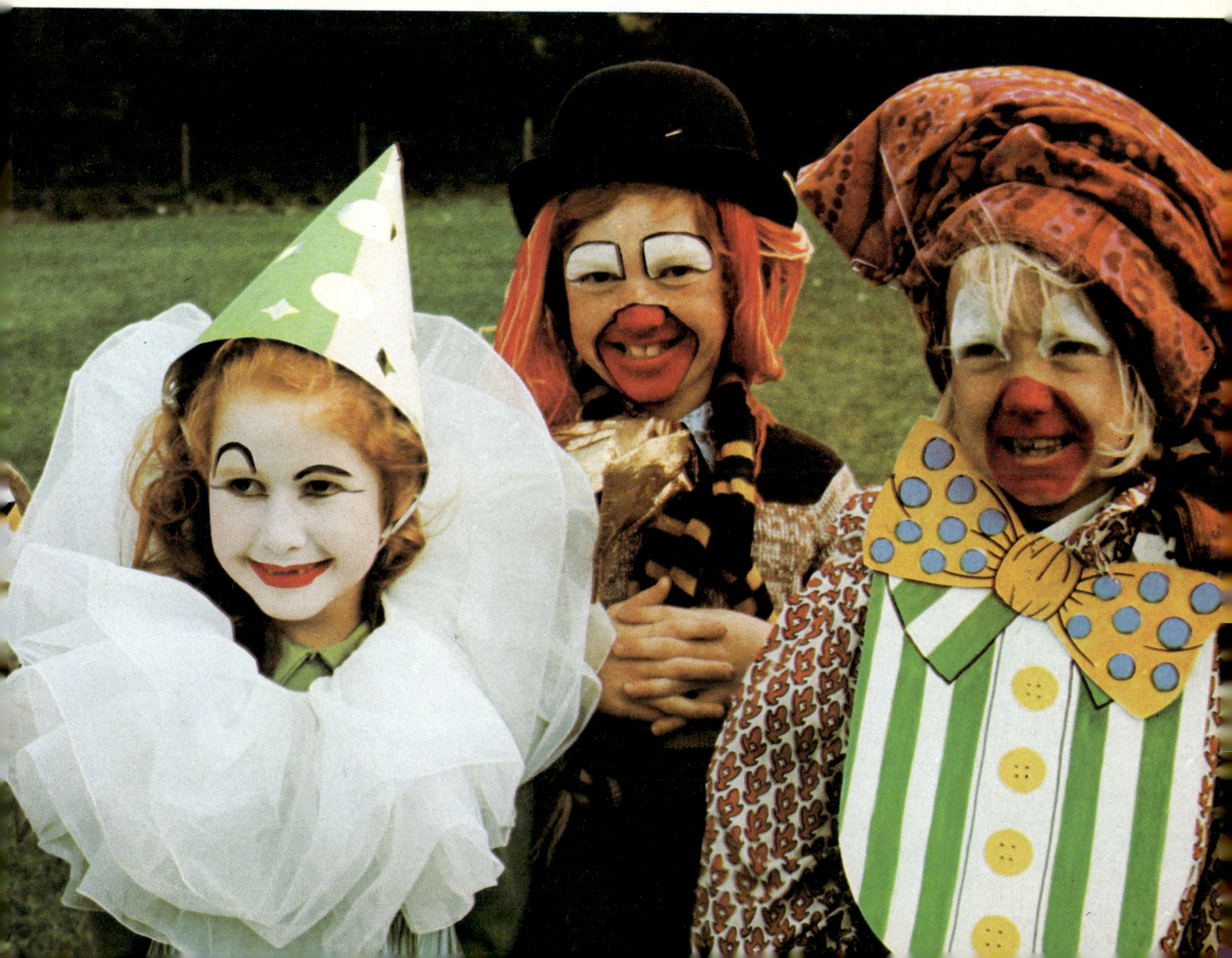

Auguste clown costumes

You will need:
(for auguste and white-face clown clothing) white card, tape, string or elastic, wool, crepe paper, sticky tape, glue, paints, or crayons.

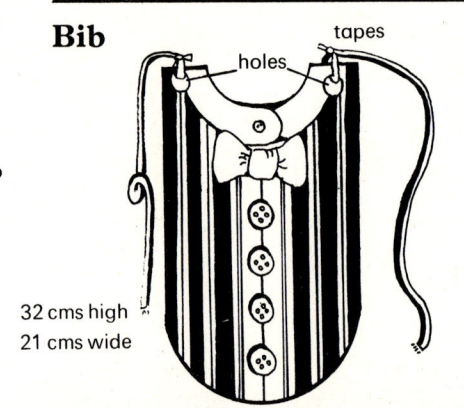

Bib
holes — tapes
32 cms high
21 cms wide

Cut a bib shape from white card. Paint on a collar, buttons, a bow tie, or other decorations.

Make small holes in the 'shoulders'. Thread tape or string through and knot it at the back. Tie the tapes round your neck.

Wig

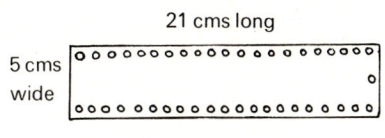

21 cms long
5 cms wide
12 mm between holes

1. Cut a strip of card. Make holes. Paint it skin colour.

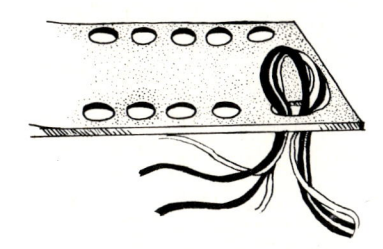

2. Cut wool into 50 cms long pieces. Fold four in half. Push folded ends through hole.

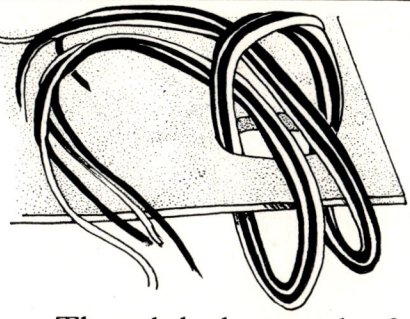

3. Thread the loose ends of wool through the loop. Pull them tight.

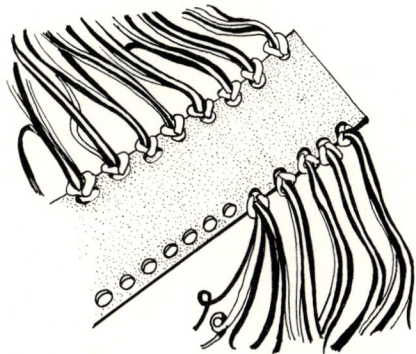

4. Do the same with all the other holes. Pull the wool to the outside of the strip.

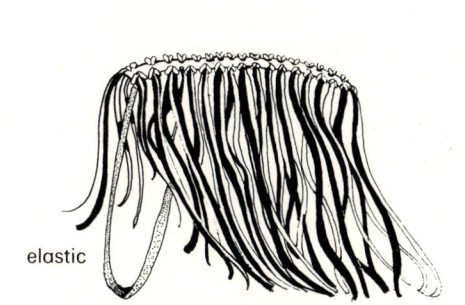

5. Fix elastic to the front, long enough to fit comfortably under your chin.

6. How to wear the wig. (You could make a stronger wig using material.

Shoes

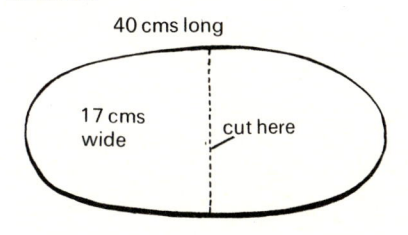

40 cms long
17 cms wide
cut here

ribbon or string laces   paint it   cardboard or crepe paper buckles and bows

1. Cut two ovals from card. Cut each oval in half.

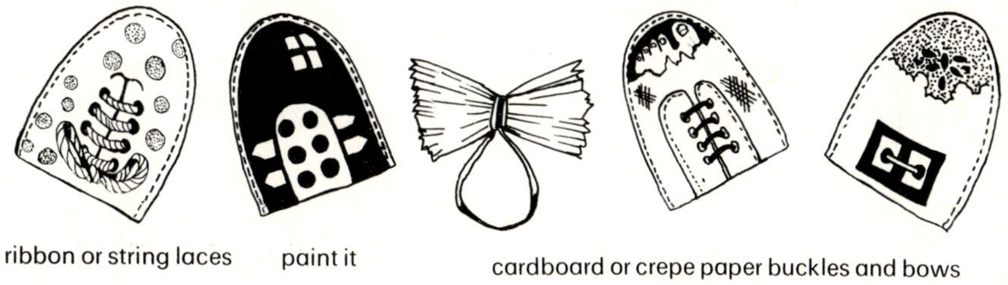

2. Paint one half of each a bright colour. Decorate it.

3. Here are some ideas. Attach decorations with string.

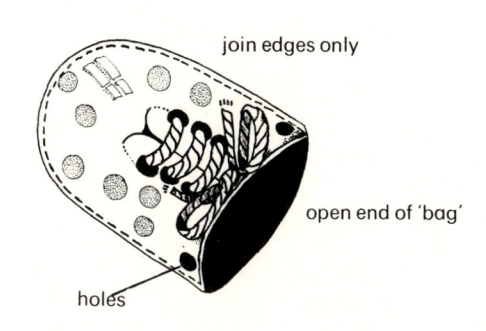

join edges only
open end of 'bag'
holes
elastic
knot

4. Glue the edges of the two halves together so they make a 'bag' for your toes. (Or sew them, using thick needle and thread). Make two holes.

5. Stuff shoes with newspaper. Put them on. Thread elastic through one hole, round your heel and through other hole. Pull tight, knot underneath.

6. Try other shaped shoes. Here are some ideas.

37

White-face clown costumes

Cone hat

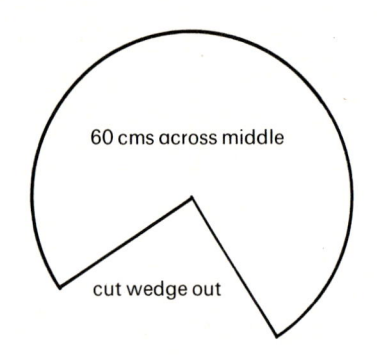

1. Cut a circle from thick white paper. Cut a wedge out of this circle.

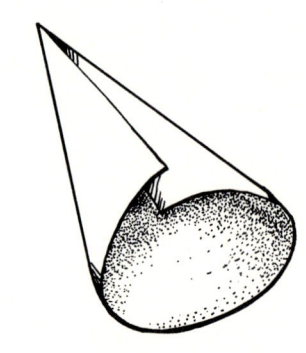

2. Make a cone. Overlap the edges till the cone fits your head. Glue the edges in place.

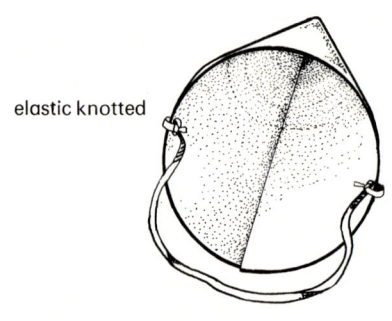

3. Fix elastic long enough to go under your chin.

4. You wear the hat with the join at the back.

Shoe decorations

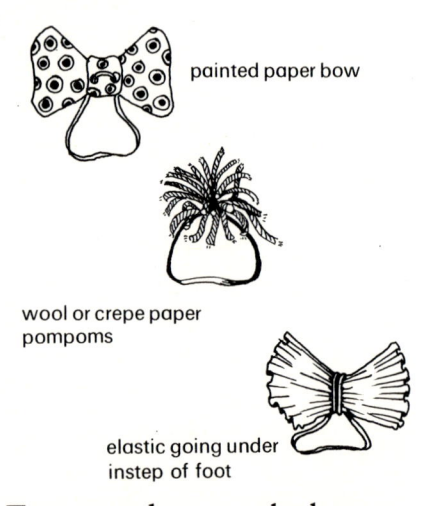

For your shoes, make bows from crepe paper or painted cardboard. Make pompoms from wool and crepe paper. Fix them to shoes with elastic.

Collar

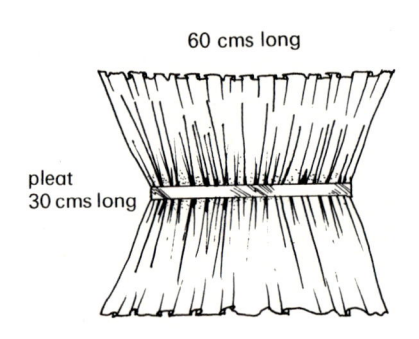

1. Cut a piece of crepe paper 40 cms by 60 cms long. Pleat it across the middle and hold the pleat in place with sticky tape.

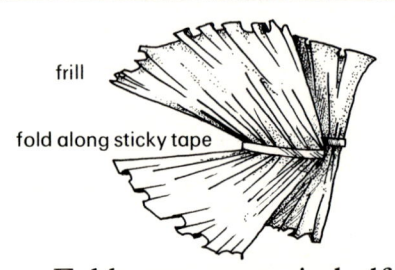

2. Fold crepe paper in half. Stretch loose end to make frill.

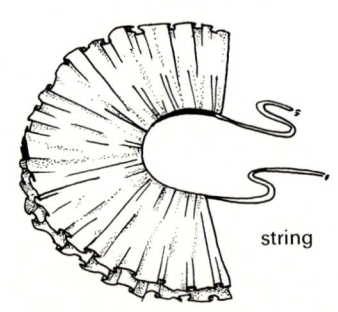

3. Attach tape or string for tying round your neck.

Clown costumes to find

A clown's clothes are a very important way of telling the audience about his character. If you want to be a clown, you must experiment with clothes until you find the right ones for the kind of clown you want to be, and practise ways of walking and behaving which match your chosen costume.

First collect all the old clothes you can find. Look for shirts, trousers, shoes, hats, scarves, coats. Look for colourful things and things you know won't fit you. At first you will want to put on everything at once. If you look in a mirror you will be surprised at how funny you look already.

Now try some experiments. If you are a small person, wear a big coat. If you are a big person, wear a small coat. Try wearing a big pair of shoes, or a pair of high-heeled shoes—a big hat or a little hat. Then practise ways of walking and behaving which you think suit your clothes. Then put together the different things which you think work well together.

Play a game with all the hats you have collected. Take them behind a curtain or door and pop out wearing a different hat each time. Pull a different face for each hat.

Clowns usually carry a few things with which they can play jokes. These are called 'props'.

Find a way of making a trick flower that squirts water.

Try making a string of sausages from old nylon tights. Stuff the tights with scraps of material or paper and tie the sausages with string.

Roll up some newspaper and bind it with sticky tape. Now you have a truncheon for hitting your clown friends without hurting them.

Circus clowns

You are in a circus. The music announces the clowns. Into the ring tumbles a noisy crowd, falling over each other in their haste to be first in. This is called the 'Charivari', an old word meaning 'hubbub'. The 'Charivari' includes both white-face clowns and augustes. It gives the clowns the chance to introduce themselves to the audience. Then a whistle sounds and the clowns are gone as quickly as they came.

The whistle is blown by the Ringmaster, who introduces the various acts and controls the running of the performance.

It is a rule in every circus that the show must never stop. To cover the gaps between the various acts while the ring staff set up the equipment, the Ringmaster signals to the 'run-in' clowns, who distract the audience from watching the work of the ring staff. 'Run-in' clowns have to be ready to dash into the ring at any moment, and so their dressing room is just behind the curtain which separates the ring from the backstage area. In American circuses this space is nick-named 'Clown Alley'. Clowns who work alone are called 'carpet clowns', perhaps because they have to carry all their equipment and some of them took to carrying it in a large carpet bag.

More often a white-face clown works with a group of augustes to perform individual acts called 'entrees'. Some entrees have been used by clowns for hundreds of years. They are known by their titles, such as 'The Broken Mirror', 'The Water Entree', 'The Nightingale', 'The Statue'. One of the most famous is 'The Barber of Seville' which shows a man having a shave. The Barber attacks him with an enormous brush and bucketsful of lather. Many clown acts include a great deal of mess, with water, powder, or a messy liquid called 'slosh'.

Often clown acts are based on special skills. There have been clowns who were talented acrobats, jugglers, and animal trainers, clowns who sang, danced, told jokes, or played musical instruments.

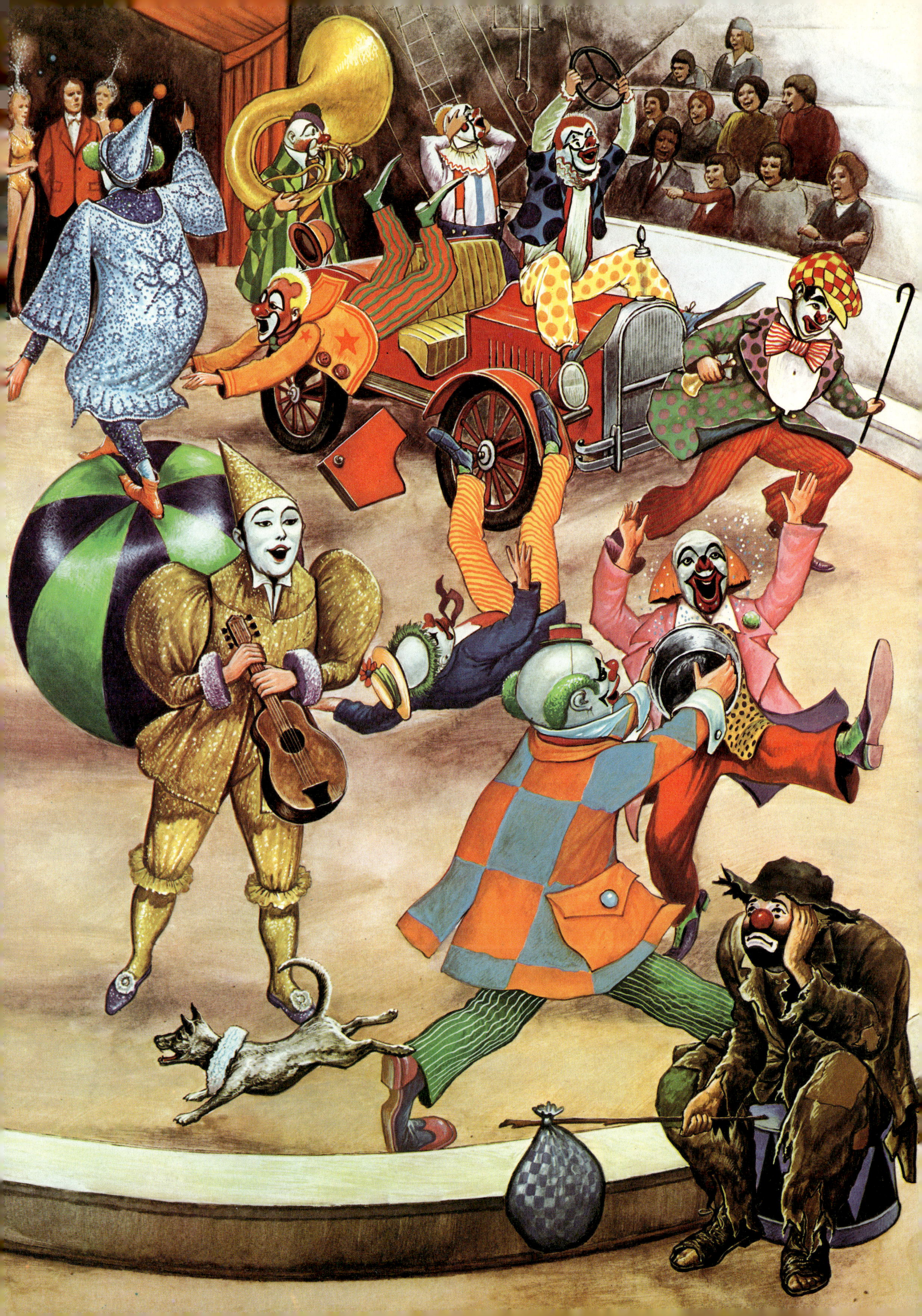

Tricks and routines

The games clowns play and the tricks they perform are called 'routines'. These are often very simple and have been passed on from one generation of clowns to the next.

Here is a simple routine for one person. Imagine you are walking down the street. Suddenly you trip. Do this by catching the instep of one foot behind the ankle of the other. (Don't catch the toe behind the ankle, or you will fall over!) Now repeat the whole movement exactly. After the second trip you stop to examine the 'thing' that has been tripping you up. You step over an imaginary object, lifting both feet very carefully. Take two more paces, looking very pleased with yourself and then trip again! The 'thing' has moved! This routine needs a lot of practice, but is very funny if you time your movements well.

Clowns very often work in pairs. Some famous clown pairs you may have seen are 'Laurel and Hardy' and 'Morecambe and Wise'. Can you think of any others? In these double acts, one clown usually appears to be sensible, and the other one plays the fool. Here are some routines for you to do with a friend.

Pretend to look into a mirror. Your friend pretends to be your 'reflection' in the mirror. The 'reflection' must copy exactly every movement you make. If you grin, so must your 'reflection'. Practise other head, arm and leg movements. Make sure every movement you both make is exactly the same. Now change round, and you be the 'reflection' of your friend.

There is a famous routine which is performed by three clowns. Clown A has a glass of water. Clown B has nothing. Clown C has a bucket. Clown A drinks the water. Clown B gargles, and Clown C spits into the bucket. Of course Clown B and C both have water in their mouths from the very beginning!

Stand with your arms behind your back. Get a friend to put his or her arms under your shoulders. Now you tell a story while your friend makes all the hand and arm movements to go with the story. Imagine you are giving a speech at school about school dinners!

Pretend to pick a flea out of the hair of one of your friends. Put it in the palm of your hand and talk to it. Give it a name, such as Fred. Announce to the audience that the flea is going to leap from one hand to the other, 'Right, Fred,' you say. 'One, two, three, jump!' The flea won't do it. You repeat your instructions and ask everyone else to shout 'jump' with you. This time the flea jumps. You ask everyone to clap. You join in with the clapping and then realise you've squashed poor Fred!

Put a large very wet hanky into the pocket of your clown costume. Put a bucket partly filled with water near you. Now start to make loud crying noises. One of your clown friends asks you what is the matter. You cry more loudly and take out the hanky to wipe your eyes and blow your nose. Now wring the hanky out into a bucket! All the water will trickle out, making loud splashing noises as it falls into the bucket!

Now put this bucket behind a chair which has a coat draped over the back so that the audience can't see behind it. Then bring out an identical looking bucket from behind the chair. You go to throw it over your audience. You say, 'Shall I?' And they shout 'No!' Again you say, 'Shall I?' Again and again they shout 'No'. But, you can't resist it and throw the contents of the bucket over them. Luckily the bucket only contains little bits of paper which you have already cut up and hidden inside. No one gets wet and everyone laughs.

Pompoms and ruffles

In France for a long time one sort of clown was more popular than any other; that was Pierrot, the sad clown of the Commedia dell'Arte. He still had a white face and wore a baggy white costume with huge black buttons, but in the 19th century he turned from a comic figure to a romantic one. Pierrot appeared in mimes and ballets. He was always in love with beautiful Columbine, but was always losing her to the more confident Harlequin.

Entertainers in England were looking for a different type of comic act from the Minstrel shows which were very popular. They decided to copy the costume of the French Pierrot. And so the first 'Pierrot Shows' began.

Apart from the costume, the English Pierrots were not at all like the French ones. They sang and danced, and told jokes to amuse their audiences. They were never sad. Their shows were performed at the sea-side, at first on simple stages on the beach, hardly big enough to take the Pierrots themselves and their piano.

During the show the Pierrots collected money from the audience, sometimes using little boys to collect it, usually in a wide-necked bottle. Once the coins were in the bottle, they couldn't be reached. When the collection had been made, the manager of the company would break the bottles and take the money. To this day, collecting money from an audience is called 'bottling'.

Eventually the most popular Pierrot companies were able to build permanent theatres in the bigger seaside towns. The shows became more and more splendid, with elaborate scenery and costumes, until the simple Pierrot Show turned into the spectacular summer shows performed today.

Many famous comedians gained their experience in the seaside Pierrot companies. It was wonderful training, for if a Pierrot could make an audience laugh, despite all the difficulties of performing there, he was a very good clown indeed.

45

Great clowns of the past

The American clown, Dan Rice was born in New York in 1823. At first he was a jockey, but he grew too big, and went to work in the local circus as a weight lifter. Then one day he saw there was a performing pig for sale. he bought it, and started his own show. Finally he became a clown and toured all over the United States of America.

The history of clowning is made up of the stories of those well-loved clowns who were so popular that tales about them live long after the clowns themselves stopped performing.

One very popular clown was an Englishman called Dicky Usher. In 1809 he announced that he would sail down the River Thames from Westminster to Waterloo Bridge in a barrel drawn by eight geese, although really the tub was towed along by a rope attached to a boat sailing far along in front. When Dicky arrived at Waterloo Bridge, he got into a cart drawn by eight tom cats to drive to the theatre where he was performing.

Perhaps the most famous American clown was Dan Rice, who is shown in the picture on the left. His act included a pig, the pig performing tricks while Dan sang and danced in between. Finally, Dan became a clown, and toured all over the United States of America. He became a very rich man.

Dan Rice wasn't the only clown to have a performing pig. The famous Duroff Brothers from Russia had a pig called 'Chuska' which had been trained to descend from a balloon by parachute. The Duroff Brothers were so popular that they even had a street in Moscow named after them.

The three Fratellini clowns were born into circus life. In fact each of them had been born while the family was touring across Europe— one in Italy, one in France and one in Russia. The trio included one white-face clown and two augustes. Their fame spread beyond the circus and in 1923 they were invited to perform their act at the Comédie Française in Paris, which is one of the most respected theatres in the world.

The greatest clowns have often received high honours. One of these was the Swiss musical clown, Grock. He loved clowns when he was a child, so when he grew up he joined a circus as an auguste clown. In South America he met the white-face clown Antonet, who became his partner for many years.

Above: the three Fratellini clowns, the white-faced Albert, and auguste clowns Paul and François with the ringmaster.

Right: the Swiss clown Grock, towards the end of his career as a clown. Grock left the circus and went to work in theatres. He was just as popular there as he had been in the circus ring. On stage he wore a huge overcoat like a tent and enormous boots. His white shirt was long and baggy, and he had great gloves with floppy fingers. Grock was a musical clown, but every instrument he tried seemed to go wrong, until he found his tiny violin and played a beautiful tune.

After many years, Grock returned to his first love, the circus ring, and toured all over Europe with his own circus. At the end of a very long and successful career, Grock finally retired in 1954. Today the 'Grock Award' is presented each year to the best clown at the International Festival of Clowning.

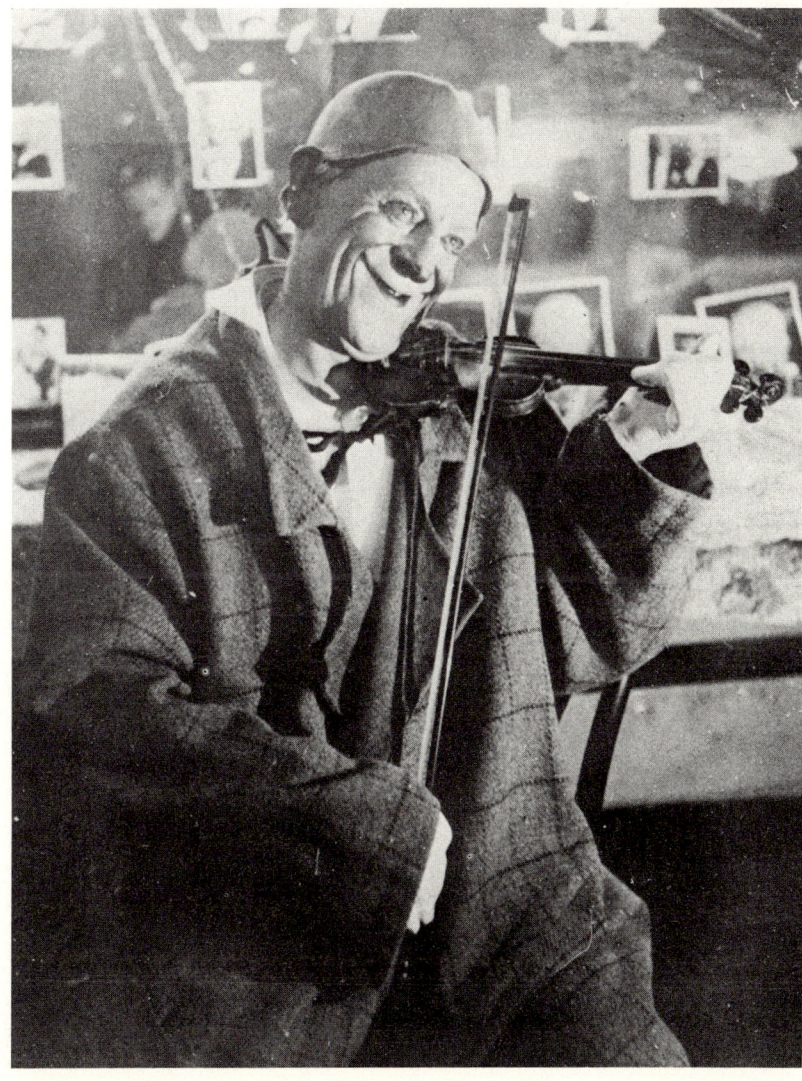

Famous clowns of today

There are now several circus schools in the world where people can learn the trade of circus clowning, and there are many talented clowns who dedicate their lives to making us laugh!

The British clowns Jacko Fosset and Little Billy delight circus audiences with their escapades—painting and decorating, hunting ducks, and going to the moon in 'Jacko's Jolly Jet'. In one routine, Jacko in flippers and snorkel goes swimming, and comes face to face with a mermaid who looks remarkably like Little Billy!

Dutch clown Henrico, with his curly hair, bright check suits and enormous boots, does all kinds of routines, from playing musical instruments to knockout routines with a teetering ladder.

French-born Charlie Cairoli plays to audiences at circuses and ice-shows and even has his own television show. His musical acts are very popular. He plays a strange assortment of instruments, including bicycle pumps and kitchen sinks! There is a picture of Charlie, with the white-face clown, Charlie Cairoli Junior, on page 52.

Above: the American auguste clown Lou Jacobs with his tiny comedy car has been a star of Barnum and Bailey's Circus in America for over 50 years.

Left: Oleg Popov, the Russian clown, putting make-up on his wife before a performance. Popov was an excellent performer on the tight-rope and slack-wire before he became a clown. He is shy and clumsy, and wins the audience's hearts at once! His costume and make-up is based on the red-haired heroes of Russian folk-tales.

Above right: the famous French mime artist, Marcel Marceau. In his clown character of 'Bip' he has shown that words can be quite unnecessary. 'Bip' can express everything through movements.

Right: Lindsay Kemp is a British mime clown. Both Marceau and Lindsay Kemp have performed all over the world. As they do not use words their clowning can be understood by people of many different nationalities.

49

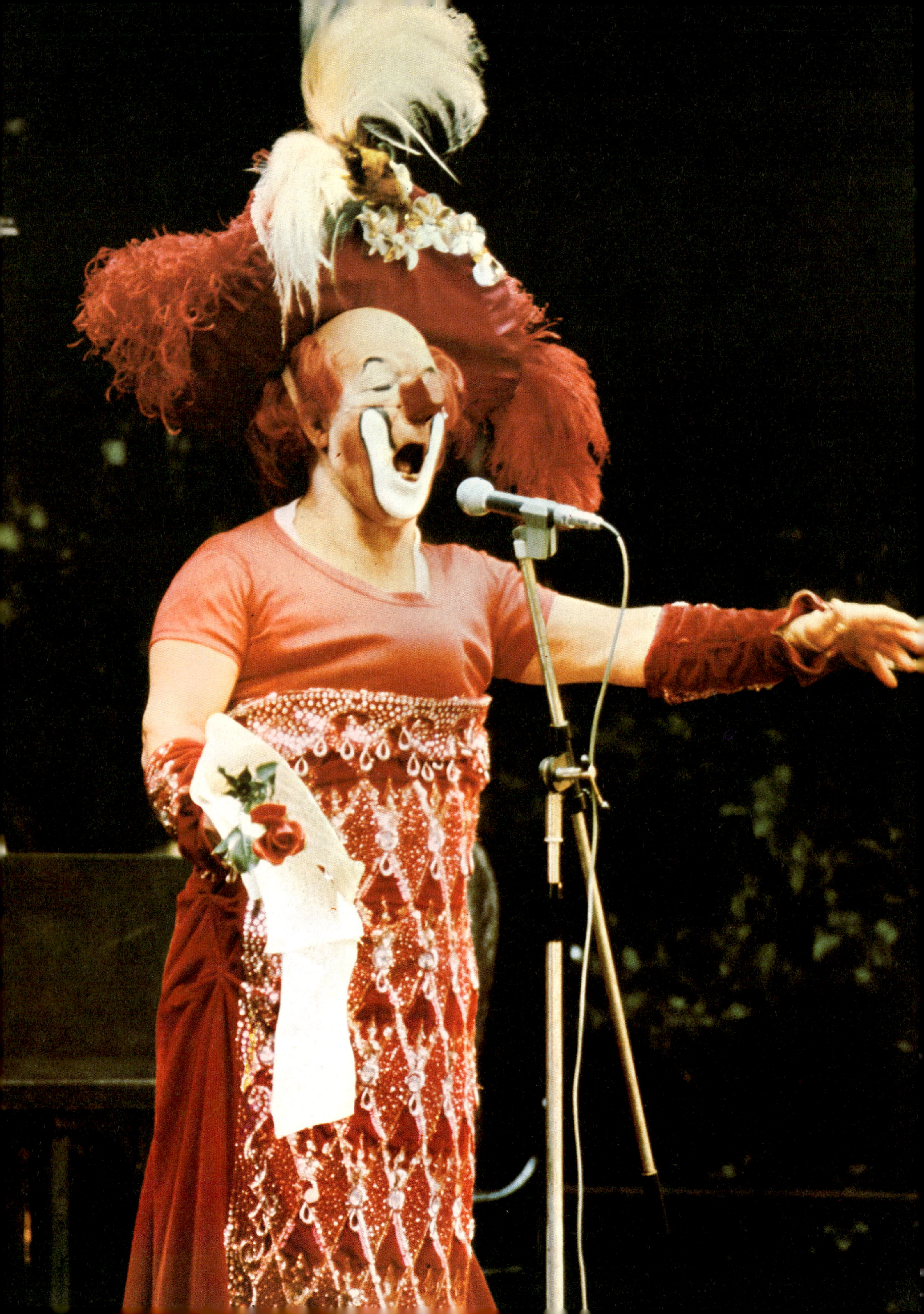

Clown acrobats and jugglers

Many clowns are talented jugglers and acrobats who pretend they are scared stiff or about to fall to make the audience laugh.

Charlie Rivel, the Spanish clown, was a famous tight-rope walker. He saw one of Charlie Chaplin's films, and, copying Chaplin's tramp character and costume, he started clowning on the tight-rope. Now he has his own auguste clown personality and is famous all over the world. He is over 80, but he still performs in circuses. His photograph is on the left.

American Emmett Kelly was a newspaper cartoonist at first. One day he drew a sad-faced tramp in a ragged suit and battered bowler hat. He often thought about this little tramp figure. By then he was working as a trapeze artist. Then one day he was asked if he would like to be a clown, and he remembered the tramp drawing again. He searched for the right clothes in junk shops, and finally he was ready. His tramp clown character is called Wearie Willy.

The East German clowns, Bubi and Jule, arrive in the ring in a donkey cart with a long pole, on top of which sits a roosting hen. The hen lays some eggs. The clowns juggle with the eggs until a few land on their heads. Then they climb above the ring and start to clean the lights high up in the Big Top. As one of them stretches out to reach the lights, he slips, but his partner catches him by his braces. They are elastic, and the clown bobs up and down like a giant yoyo!

The clown Fattini always staggers into the ring and interrupts the show. He is very drunk but insists on climbing a long 12-metre pole. When he gets to the top he balances on his head and does other acrobatic tricks on the swaying pole, before he slides headfirst down to the ground!

Once Swiss clown Pio Nock's act nearly ended in tragedy. He was tight-rope walking while underneath him was a cage of 17 lions. At one performance he slipped, but landed in the ring with no broken bones, and managed to get out of the cage before the lions realised what had happened!

Above: Emmett Kelly as the tramp clown 'Wearie Willy'. While other clowns dash about the ring, Willy ambles about, lost in his own world, a contrast to all the hustle and bustle around him.

Below: The balancing act 'The Herculeans' are world champion acrobats. They are led by Johnny Hutch, at 64 the oldest tumbler in Europe.

Clowning families

In clowning it is very important that the timing is perfect. Every clown must be able to rely on his partner to do the act as it was rehearsed, or the comic acrobatics may end in an accident. The longer a group of clowns works together and the better they know each other, the better the timing is likely to be.

Some of the most famous clown troupes have been families who work together all their lives. Clown acts are often handed down from one generation of a family to the next. Some families have been clowns for over 100 years. This way the experience of clowning is not lost when one particular clown retires, but can be handed on and the traditional forms of comedy kept alive. Some of the wonderful acts designed by the Fratellini troupe are still being performed by Annie Fratellini, the grand-daughter of the auguste clown Paul Fratellini.

Below: Charlie Cairoli in a well-known family partnership. The sequin-covered white-face clown with Charlie is in fact his son, Charlie Junior.

Other famous clowns are also members of clowning families. For example Coco's son, Michael still wears his father's costume and make-up and runs a highly successful clown troupe in America, while brother Sascha has become a white-face clown and performs all over the world.

Not only was Charlie Rivel's father a clown, but his brothers were clowns too, and all three of Charlie's sons became clowns in their turn!

In the early history of the theatre it was not thought proper for ladies to go to places of entertainment alone, never mind perform in them. But women soon proved that they could be just as good as men at making people laugh.

For hundreds of years clown troupes have included one or two pretty girls as a contrast to the grotesque and bumbling clowns, such as Columbine in the Harlequinade. Modern circus clowns still include women.

The first lady clown in the circus was probably Elizabeth Sylvester, who worked in Pablo Franque's Circus in England in 1875. At the turn of the century there was also a Frenchwoman who took the Chinese name of Cha-U-Kao to make Parisian audiences laugh.

Today women are working in all branches of clowning—in theatre, and circuses, as white-face clowns, like Barbarina and Suki in England, or as augustes like England's Cath Carpenter, who with her husband forms the team of Rolo and Shandy with Cath as the tramp auguste.

Women can also become clown mimes, like the Belgian female mime troupe Sabbatini.

Above: white-face clown Suki of the Clown Cavalcade troupe in England. She uses mime and dance as well as traditional slap-stick acts with her clown partners.

Below: Cocatina, grand-daughter of the famous clown Coco.

English white-faced clown Brinarno, of Clown Cavalcade, performs a juggling act.

Clown exercises and a clown band

A clown needs control of both sides of his body in order to be able to juggle, tumble or do any other acrobatic acts. Here are some exercises to make both halves of your body work equally well.
1. Hold your nose with your left hand and your left ear with your right hand. Now change over so that the right hand holds the nose and the left hand holds the right ear. Do it slowly at first, then faster and faster. Don't move your head, only your hands.
2. Pat your head with your right hand and rub your stomach in a circular movement with your left hand. Then change round—your left hand on your head and right hand rubbing your stomach.
3. Stand on one leg with your other foot tucked into your knee, like a stork. Stretch your arms out to the sides, and remember to breathe or you'll fall over! Concentrate on a point on a wall to help you balance. Now shut your eyes. Think hard of the same point on the wall and remember to breathe!
4. Throw a ball against a wall with your right hand. Catch it with your left. Throw it back with your left and catch it with your right. Do the same thing throwing the ball in the air, low at first, and then higher and higher.

1. Practise your sense of rhythm. Clap your hands slowly and regularly. Get a friend to join in, clapping on exactly the same beat as you. Then get them to clap in between your claps—this is called on the 'off-beat'.
2. Walk round the room. Usually the leg on one side of your body swings with the arm on the opposite side (that is, your right leg and your left arm). Now make your right arm swing with your right leg and left arm with the left leg.
3. For your clown musical instruments use anything that makes a good loud noise—tin lids, combs and paper, boxes of dried peas or small stones—anything you can think of. Practise using them with fast and slow rhythm.
4. Now for your clown band! One clown starts to play. The next joins in, either playing on or off the beat. Then the next and next, until everyone is playing. Take it in turns to be the conductor and make the band play loudly or quietly, slow them down or speed them up.
5. Build up the rhythm and the noise, till it is very fast and loud. Then all collapse in a heap!

Clowns in films

When films were invented in the 1890s many clowns were able to bring the skills they had learnt in the theatre into the cinema.

Early comedy films were like circus routines. The films were short, with simple plots and characters. Each film could be seen by millions of people. There was no spoken dialogue, only occasional captions, so language was no problem and the films could be shown easily in foreign countries. In fact, the experts thought that the very best comedy films needed no captions to explain the action at all.

Soon everybody knew the leading cinema clowns. Each clown had a special personality all his own; Harry Langdon had a round baby face, Chester Conklin had crossed eyes, Fatty Arbuckle was as fat as a barrel, Harold Lloyd performed terrifying stunts in his comedy routines, the Keystone Cops were famous for their hair-raising car chases.

The pale make-up the clowns had to wear in the early films so that their faces would show up for the camera, made them look very like their ancestors, the white-face clowns from the circus and the theatre.

Then films began to use sound. Words as well as funny situations could be used to make people laugh. Some clowns worked in groups, like the Marx Brothers, or the Three Stooges. There were many famous clown partnerships, like Stan Laurel and Oliver Hardy, Bud Abbot and Lou Costello, and Dean Martin and Jerry Lewis. Sound also led to the use of 'catch phrases'— words that were used in every film—like Oliver Hardy's 'Here's another fine mess you've got me into'.

The cinema still has its own clowns like Danny Kaye, Woody Allen, Jacques Tati, Fernandel, and the famous 'Carry On' team.

Now, through television, the early comedy films are being shown again, and a whole new generation of children are laughing at Charlie Chaplin and his friends, just as children did 70 years ago.

Left: Charlie Chaplin's funny tramp figure was loved all over the world.
Below: Buster Keaton with his famous 'stone face' that never smiled.

Below: the Marx Brothers from left to right, Harpo, Chico and Groucho. Their musical routines were very famous.
Bottom: the famous comedy team of English Stan Laurel and American Oliver 'Babe' Hardy.

A clown routine for two

This routine is called 'The Broken Mirror', and it has been performed for over 100 years. It was made famous by the French clowns, the Fratellinis. We have called the white-face clown Pipo and the auguste Rum, after two famous clowns who performed the routine in the 1950s.

You will need 2 lengths of material or crepe paper for togas (old white sheets would be good), 2 dusters, a glass of orange squash, a large frame for the mirror which you can balance on the seat of a chair. Make it out of cardboard and decorate it. You can practise the routine easily by standing on either side of an open window or door.

The routine:
PIPO I'm very pleased with myself today. I've been offered a leading part in the play 'Julius Caesar', so now I must practise my words and actions. Rum!
RUM What is it?
PIPO Fetch me that big glass from my dressing room.
RUM You want a glass?
PIPO Yes, I want a glass.
Rum goes and comes back with a glass of orange juice.
PIPO Not that sort of glass, you fool. I want a looking glass, a mirror, so that I can see myself. Fetch me a large mirror, and be careful you don't drop it. I must go and put on my costume.
Pipo goes off. Rum goes to fetch the mirror. There is the sound of a crash. Rum enters carrying the frame of a mirror.
RUM What shall I do? Pipo will be furious! I know, I'll pretend to be his reflection. If I wear a costume like his and stand behind the mirror he won't notice a thing.
Hurriedly he drapes a sheet round himself and stands behind the mirror, just as Pipo appears also wearing a sheet.
PIPO Ah, there's the mirror.
He strikes a pose and looks at the mirror. Rum copies him.
PIPO That's strange, I thought I was much better looking than that! It must be the mirror.
Pipo crosses his arms, thoughtfully puts his hand to his chin. Rum copies him. Pipo turns round suspiciously, then waves and smiles. Again Rum copies him.
PIPO Perhaps the mirror needs polishing.
He pulls a duster from his pocket and polishes the glass. Rum does the same. Their hands meet.
PIPO I don't understand this at all. Perhaps I need a drink.
He fetches the glass of orange juice. Standing sideways to the mirror he takes a drink. Rum doesn't have a glass of his own, so he reaches through the frame and takes the glass from Pipo. He hands the empty glass back to Pipo who looks at him in surprise.
PIPO What's this? I should have guessed! Rum's been playing a trick on me. Come back here!
RUM I didn't mean any harm, really I didn't!
PIPO You wait till I catch you!
Rum runs away and Pipo chases after him.

58

A balancing act

You need: a parasol or umbrella, a ball that isn't too heavy, some string, drawing pins.

1. Attach one end of the string to the ball. Pin the other end to the top of the umbrella. Make sure the string is short enough to allow the ball to hang on top of the opened umbrella. It mustn't hang over the edge.
2. Announce to your audience that you will show them a wonderful balancing act. Hold the umbrella upright. Spin the handle. The speed of the turning umbrella will make it look as though you are really balancing the ball on the umbrella.
3. Take a bow before the audience realises that you have been fooling them!

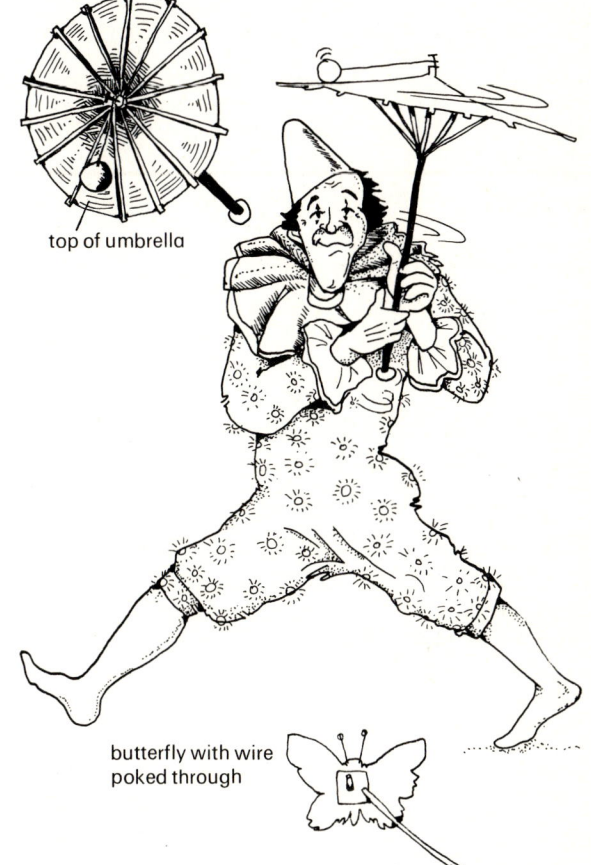

The butterfly chase

You need: cardboard, paints, crayons or felt markers, wire, sticky tape, a stick and a toy gun.

1. Cut a butterfly shape out of cardboard and paint it in bright colours.
2. Make a circle of wire big enough to go round your head. Cover the join where the circle meets with the sticky tape.
3. Straighten the remaining wire out and attach the end to the butterfly. There should be at least 23 cms between the circle and the butterfly.
4. Put the circle of wire on your head with the butterfly out in front of you.

The routine: the clown is determined to catch the butterfly for his collection, but however fast he runs he cannot catch it. He tries to hit it with a stick, but he cannot reach it. (If you have a fishing net you could try to catch the butterfly with that.) Finally the clown gets his gun and decides to shoot the butterfly. He holds the gun with two hands out in front of him and pulls the trigger, but he misses the butterfly and shoots himself. He falls to the ground, but he gets up in time to stop the audience worrying—and to take his applause.

Today and tomorrow

Throughout history the clown has changed how he looks and acts to suit the audiences of his day. Greek and Roman clowns performed for thousands of people in huge arenas. Jesters played for just a handful of people at the royal palace. When clowns could no longer earn their living working for rich families, they started entertaining new audiences in theatres and circuses. Today clowns also work on television where they can be seen by thousands of people at one time.

Nowadays you see clowns in all kinds of places! Perhaps a company of clowns has visited your school, given a show in your local park, in front of shops or even in church. Clowns perform wherever they can find an audience.

To make people laugh, clowns have told jokes, or not said a word, sung and danced, used water, foam and mess of all kinds. Now they use modern science to make more and more elaborate equipment for themselves, from comedy cars which drive themselves to exploding cookers and all sorts of splendid tricks and effects. Some clowns have even borrowed techniques from electronics and films.

If some day space travel makes it possible for people to live on planets millions of kilometres away, clowns are sure to equip themselves with comedy space suits and intergalactic jokes—all ready to amuse a new audience. I expect clowns will find a way to make Martians laugh too!

Below, left: Clowns may not wear traditional costumes. At Blackpool Tower Circus in England, Charlie Cairoli and Charlie Junior are just as funny wearing only overalls.
Far left: English comic Ken Dodd uses his skills as a clown even in the middle of a television interview.
Below: Clowns perform wherever they find an audience. English clowns Antonio and Bazzo as Leo the Lion, of Clown Cavalcade, perform on the pavement outside shops.

Index

acrobats 25, 28, 29, 32, 40, 41, 46, 50, 51, 54, 55
American clowns 46, 48, 49, 51
animal trainers 12, 13, 28, 29, 41
auguste clowns 32-37, 39-43, 46-55, 58-61

Balinese clowns 7
Belgian clowns 53
British clowns 24-31, 33, 46, 48, 49, 51-54, 56, 60, 61
Burmese clowns 7

carpet clowns 40
Charivari 40, 41
Chinese clowns 6, 7
circus 28-33, 40, 41, 46-53
circus owners
    Astley (Philip) 28, 29
    Barnum 29, 49
    Ducrow (Andrew) 29
    Hughes (Charles) 29
    Ricketts (Bill) 29
Clown Alley 40
clown families 52, 53
clowns on horseback 28, 29
Commedia dell' Arte 22, 23, 25, 44
costume 22, 23, 25, 30-33, 36-39

Clowns and clown characters
Abbot (Bud) and Costello (Lou) 56
Allen (Woody) 56
Antonet 46
Antonio 33, 61
Arlecchino (also Harlequin) 22-27, 44

Barbarina 53
Bazzo 33, 61
Belling (Tom) 32
Bip 49
Brighella 22, 23
Brinarno 54
Bubi and Jule 51
Buster Keaton 57

Cairoli (Charlie) 48, 52, 60, 61
Cairoli (Charlie, Junior) 30, 48, 52, 61
Captain 22, 23
Carpenter (Cath) 53
'Carry On' comedy team 56
Chaplin (Charlie) 51, 56, 57
Cha-U-Kao 53
Cicirrus 8, 9, 18
Clown 24, 25, 26, 27
Clown Cavalcade 33, 53, 54, 61
Cocatina 53

court clowns and jesters 6-9, 18, 19, 60

Dutch clowns 48

Eastern clowns 6, 7
East German clowns 51
Emperor's clowns 6, 7
English clowns *see* British clowns
entrées (*see* tricks and routines)

fairground clowns 12, 13
film clowns 56, 57
French clowns 47, 48, 49

Greek clowns 8, 9, 60

Harlequinade 24-27, 53

Italian clowns 22, 23

jesters *see* court clowns and jesters
jugglers 40, 41, 51, 54, 55

legends 14-17

make-up 30-35
Malayan clowns 7

Coco 32, 33, 52
Columbine 23, 24, 26, 27, 44, 53
Conklin (Chester) 56
Costello (Lou) 56
Cowley (Richard) 21

Davide 30, 31
Doctor 22, 23
Dodd (Ken) 60, 61
Ducrow (John) 29
Duroff Brothers 46

Eulenspiegel (Till) 16, 17

Fattini 51
Fatty Arbuckle 56
Fernandel 56
Flexmore (Richard) 30
Fosset (Jacko) 48
Fratellinis 46, 47, 52

Giufa 17
Goodfellow (Robin) 17
Grimaldi (Joseph) 24, 25, 30
Grock 46, 47
Gros-Guillaume (Fat William) 30

Hardy (Oliver) 56, 57

marottes 18
masks 8-11
merry councillors 18
mime 49, 53
motley 18
mummers 12, 13
musical clowns 40, 46-48, 52, 57

pantomime 25
Pierrot shows 44, 45

Ringmaster 40-41
Roman clowns 8, 9, 60
routines 40-43, 54, 55, 58, 59
Royal Amphitheatre 28, 29
run-in clowns 40
Russian clowns 46, 48, 49

Shakespeare's clowns 20-21
South East Asian clowns 7
Spanish clowns 50, 51
Swiss clowns 46, 47, 51

tricks *see* routines

white-face clowns 30, 31, 33-35, 38-41, 46-55, 58-61
women clowns 52, 53

Harlequin *see* Arlecchino
Henrico 48
Herculeans 51
Hudson (Jeffery) 18, 19

Jacobs (Lou) 48, 49
Jehan 18
Jule 51

Kartala 7
Kaye (Danny) 56
Keaton *see* Buster
Kelly (Emmett) 51
Kemp (Lindsay) 49
Kemp (Will) 21
Keystone Cops 56

Langdon (Harry) 56
Laurel (Stan) and Hardy (Oliver) 56, 57
Leno (Dan) 25
Lewis (Jerry) 56
Little Billy 48
Lloyd (Harold) 56

Marceau (Marcel) 49
Martin (Dean) and Lewis (Jerry) 56
Marx Brothers 56, 57

Matthews (Tom) 25
Mr Merryman 29

Nasr Ed-Din 14, 15
Nock (Pio) 51

Pantalone (also Pantaloon) 22-27
Penasar 7
Philemon 9
Pierrot 23, 24, 25, 44, 45
Pipo 58
Popov 48, 49

Pulcinello 22, 23, 25
Punch 25

Rice (Dan) 46
Rivel (Charlie) 50, 51, 52
Rolo and Shandy 53
Rum 58

Sabbatini 53
Shandy 53
Stupidus 8, 9
Suki 53

Sylvester (Elizabeth) 53

Tati (Jacques) 56
Triboulet 18

Usher (Dicky) 46

Wearie Willy 51

YuSze 7

Zappo 33

Acknowledgements

Edited by:
Beverley Birch

Artists:
Kim Blundell 3, 8-9 top, 11, 14-17, 26-27, 36-39, 42-43, 55, 58-59
Fiona French cover, 4-7, 18-23
George Thompson 8-9 bottom, 12-13, 24, 28-29, 40-41, 44-45

Photographs:
Nick Birch 10, 30, 31, 33 right, 34-35, 36, 52, 53 top, 54, 60-61 middle and right
Camera Press (Nick de Morgoli) 48-49 top middle
Circus World Museum, Baraboo, Wisconsin 46, 51 top
Ronald Grant 25 bottom, 57 top left
Kobal Collection 57 bottom
Keystone 32, 33 middle, 53 bottom
Mander and Mitchenson 25 top
Neil Maurer 51 bottom
National Film Archives 57 top right
Rene Dazy 47
Rex Features Ltd 50, 56
Society for Cultural Relations with USSR 48
Vaceslav Stanuga 49 bottom
T.V. Times 60 left
Reg Wilson 49 top

Picture Research:
Elizabeth Ogilvie

Design consultant:
Laurence Bradbury

Chris Harris activities: 39, 42-43, 55

Teacher Panel:
Penny Anderson
Stephen Harley
David Winters